POCKET

TORONTO

TOP SIGHTS • LOCAL EXPERIENCES

LIZA PRADO

Contents

Plan Your Trip 4

Welcome to Toronto............4

Top Sights........................6

Eating 10

Entertainment..................12

Drinking & Nightlife..........14

Festivals..........................15

Shopping.........................16

Freebies 17

For Kids 18

LGBTIQ+ 19

Four Perfect Days............20

Need to Know 22

Toronto Neighborhoods 24

CN Tower (p44)
YELENA RODRIGUEZ MENA/EYEEM/GETTY IMAGES ©

Explore Toronto 27

Waterfront 29

Entertainment & Financial Districts 43

Old Town, Corktown & Distillery District 59

Downtown Yonge 75

Kensington Market & Chinatown 91

Yorkville & the Annex 103

West End 117

East Toronto & Rosedale 131

Worth a Trip

Niagara Falls 142

Survival Guide 147

Before You Go 148

Arriving in Toronto 149

Getting Around 150

Essential Information 152

Index 156

Special Features

Harbourfront Centre 30

Toronto Islands 40

CN Tower 44

St Lawrence Market Complex 60

Tommy Thompson Park 72

Elgin & Winter Garden Theatre 76

Art Gallery of Ontario 92

Royal Ontario Museum 104

High Park 118

Evergreen Brick Works 132

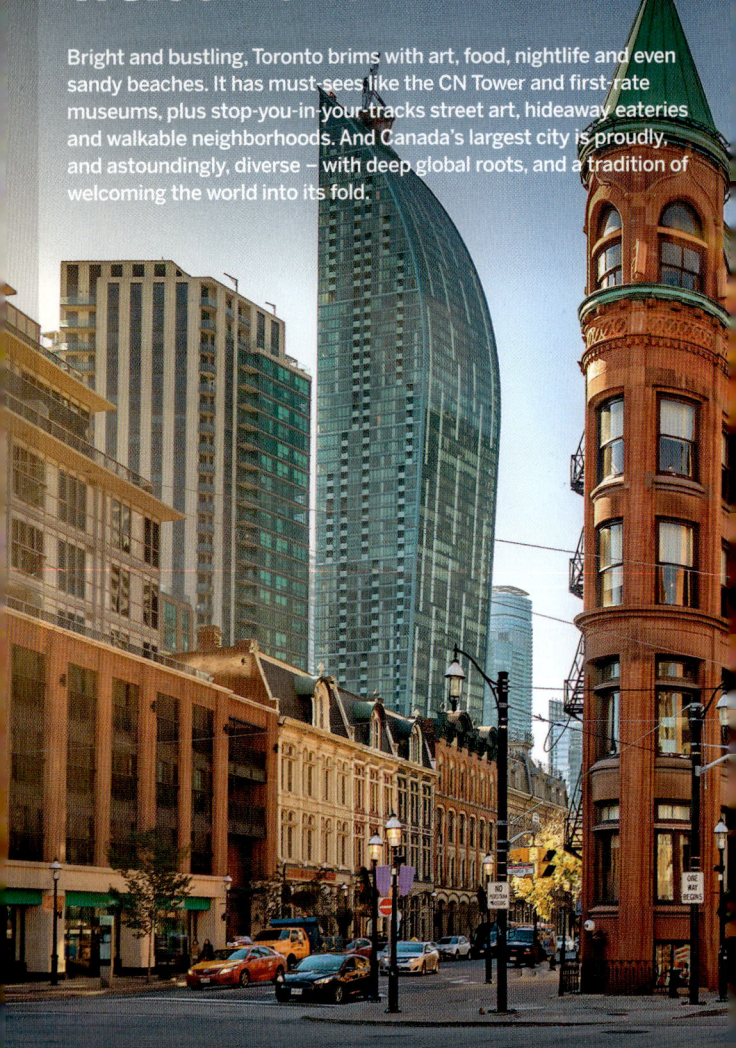

Welcome to Toronto

Bright and bustling, Toronto brims with art, food, nightlife and even sandy beaches. It has must-sees like the CN Tower and first-rate museums, plus stop-you-in-your-tracks street art, hideaway eateries and walkable neighborhoods. And Canada's largest city is proudly, and astoundingly, diverse – with deep global roots, and a tradition of welcoming the world into its fold.

Flatiron Building (p65)
DIEGO GRANDI/SHUTTERSTOCK ©

Top Sights

CN Tower
Toronto's iconic, must-see tower. **p44**

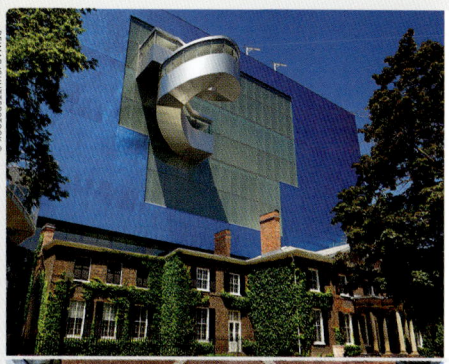

Art Gallery of Ontario
Stunning Gehry-designed art museum. **p92**

St Lawrence Market Complex
Historic farmers market and more. **p60**

Niagara Falls
Powerful and awe-inspiring waterfalls. **p142**

Plan Your Trip Top Sights

Plan Your Trip Top Sights

Elgin & Winter Garden Theatre
Beautifully restored double-decker theater. **p76**

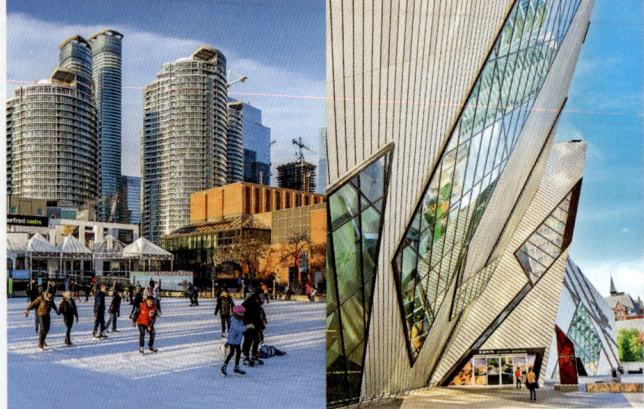

Harbourfront Centre
Impressive waterfront cultural complex. **p30**

Royal Ontario Museum
Toronto's biggest and best museum. **p104**

Evergreen Brick Works
Brick factory turned green oasis. **p132**

Toronto Islands
Lovely island escape in Toronto. **p40**

High Park
Arguably Toronto's finest public park. **p118**

Tommy Thompson Park
Unexpected urban nature reserve. **p72**

Eating

Nowhere is Toronto's multiculturalism more thrilling than in its restaurants. You'll find everything from Korean walnut cakes and sweat-inducing Thai curries to good ol' Canuck pancakes with peameal bacon and maple syrup. Fusion food is hot: traditional Western recipes are spiked with zingy Eastern ingredients, while British influences linger with fizzy lunchtime pints and formal afternoon tea.

Global Eats

Toronto has more than 7000 restaurants, representing a phenomenal range of tastes, cultures and experiences. Most neighborhoods are known for a certain scene – there's fine dining in the financial district, and hole-in-the-wall eats and homegrown talent in Kensington Market and Chinatown – but the truth is there's great food from around the world in every corner of Toronto. If ever there was a place to explore, graze and experiment, this is it.

Fine Dining

Toronto is deep into the fine dining and celebrity chef scene. Restaurants are stylish and exclusive, with idiosyncratic techniques and ingredients, and usually a menu of creative cocktails. A splurge perhaps, but always Instagram-worthy.

Food Halls

Can't decide what to eat or where to go? Dining halls may be the answer, featuring a variety of first-rate cuisines, with counter service and communal tables, and a relaxed but lively ambience. They're uber-popular and popping up all over town; Assembly Chef's Hall (pictured; p52) is a fine place to start.

Best Budget Eats

House of Gourmet No-frills restaurant with a dizzying number of Hong Kong–style dishes. (p96)

Seven Lives Standing-room-only place serving the best fish tacos in town. (p97)

Otto's Bierhalle Brats, beer and communal tables evoke Oktoberfest year-round. (p122)

Annex Food Hall Industrial-chic food court with eateries from vegan to Bangkok-style street food. (p110)

Best Fine Dining

Buca Artisanal nose-to-tail Italian served in an upscale setting, soaring ceilings and all. (p53)

Lee Mid-century Modern–inspired dining room with creative Asian plates meant to be shared. (p53)

Ruby Watchco Different nightly menu of farm-to-table comfort food. (p140)

Richmond Station Streamlined restaurant with an eclectic menu of beautifully presented dishes. (p53)

Best Specialty Eats

Pow Wow Café Fry-bread tacos are the specialty at this cozy Ojibwe eatery. (p97)

Okonomi House Simple restaurant serving *okonomiyaki* (stuffed Japanese cabbage pancakes). (p83)

Chef's House Culinary students work the front and back of this upscale restaurant. (p67)

Dipped Donuts Tiny bakery serving fancy doughnuts with surprising toppings. (p98)

A Taste of the World

Quirky, well-qualified guides lead offbeat **tours** (☎416-923-6813; www.torontowalks bikes.com; 2-3½hr tours $25-50) of Toronto's nooks and crannies, usually with a foodie focus, but also including ghost hunting.

Entertainment

As you might have guessed, there's always something going on in Toronto, from jazz and art-house cinema to offbeat theater, opera, punk rock, and hockey. In summer, free festivals and outdoor concerts are the norm, but Toronto's live-music scene keeps grooving year-round.

Theater

Long winter months indoors are conducive to the creation and performance of theatrical works. This, and Toronto's relative proximity to Broadway and cosmopolitan Montréal, help sustain the city's reputation as a theater-maker's playground. Broadway and off-Broadway musicals and plays pack theaters around the Entertainment District and Yonge & Dundas Sq. There are numerous smaller venues and vibrant young production companies around town too.

Live Music

Dust off your Iggy Pop T-shirt, don your Docs and hit the pit. Alt-rock, metal, ska, punk and funk – Toronto has a thriving live-music scene. Bebop, smoky swamp blues, classical and acoustic balladry provide some alternatives. Expect to pay anywhere from nothing to a few dollars on weeknights, up to $20 for weekend acts.

Ticketing

In an effort to promote arts and culture, many venues and events operate a 'Pay What You Can' (PWYC) policy: admission is free or by donation – give what you think is reasonable. Otherwise, Ticketmaster (www.ticketmaster.ca) sells tickets for major concerts, sporting matches and events.

Best Iconic Experiences

Elgin & Winter Garden Theatre Historic double-decker theater with big Broadway shows. (pictured; p76)

Horseshoe Tavern Legendary stage for indie bands. (p99)

COLIN WOODS/SHUTTERSTOCK ©

Toronto Maple Leafs Fiery fans and sold-out games make watching the Leafs unforgettable. (p57)

Second City Toronto Nightly improv and sketch comedy at an iconic comic stomping ground. (p55)

Best Live Music

Reservoir Lounge Longtime 'it' spot for jazz and blues. (p69)

Rex Nightly jazz and blues, from traditional to experimental. (p100)

Dakota Tavern Country-music joint with a sweet bluegrass brunch. (p127)

Best Theater

Royal Alexandra Theatre Impressive 1907 theater staging big-ticket musicals. (p56)

Soulpepper Theater company producing plays focused on the diversity of the Canadian experience. (p69)

Shakespeare in High Park Outdoor Shakespeare in one of Toronto's prettiest parks. (p119)

Best Cinemas

TIFF Bell Lightbox Magnificent cinema complex screening independent films year-round. (p55)

Hot Docs Ted Rogers Cinema Art deco theater showcasing documentaries and off-the-beaten-track films. (p113)

Entertainment Resources

blogTO (www.blogto.com) Up-to-date info on local happenings.

Now (nowtoronto.com) Alt-culture and live-music listings.

Tourism Toronto (www.seetorontonow.com) Official tourism website with events listings.

Drinking & Nightlife

Toronto's drinking scene embraces everything from gritty dive bars to sky-high cocktail lounges, plus a clubbing scene that centers on the Entertainment District. Strict bylaws prohibit smoking indoors in public spaces, although some patios allow it. Taps start flowing around midday and last call hovers around 2am.

TRPHOTOS/SHUTTERSTOCK ©

Best Bars

Bar Raval Magnificent Gaudí-inspired bar serving small Spanish plates, too. (p124)

Oxley Upscale British pub with Victorian decor and glitzy clientele. (p112)

Drake Hotel Smart rooftop bar and hipster underground music venue in the West End. (p125)

O'Grady's Irish pub popular for its patio and its Dirty Bingo Nights, hosted by drag queens. (p86)

Best Breweries

Bellwoods Brewery Award-winning beers, gourmet small plates and a hipster vibe in a two-story brewery. (p125)

Rorschach Brewing Co Century-old house turned brewery, with two patios and an ever-changing menu of beers. (p73)

Mill Street Brewery Distillery District brewery in a Victorian-era factory with over a dozen craft brews on tap. (p68)

Best City Views

Rooftop Floor-to-ceiling windows and a wraparound patio on a, yes, spectacular rooftop. (p140)

One Eighty Glitzy bar with Toronto's highest licensed patio – 51 floors up! (p87)

Against the Grain Urban Tavern Lakefront views from a spacious patio. (p39)

Best Quirky & Unusual

Storm Crow Manor Sci-fi-themed bar with dungeon masters on staff. (p87)

Snakes & Lattes More than 1000 board games plus an eclectic drink menu. (p126)

Festivals

Toronto loves festivals! Summer months are especially busy, but count on events year-round. Arts, food and culture festivals are especially popular, including the Toronto Film Festival and Pride Toronto. Others celebrate theater, music, neighborhoods, historical events and more. Check local calendars for festivals taking place during your stay.

SHAWN GOLDBERG/SHUTTERSTOCK ©

Best Performing Arts Festivals

Toronto Fringe Festival (416-966-1062; http://fringetoronto.com; $13; early Jul) Theater festival featuring more than 150 productions chosen by lottery.

Luminato (416-368-4849; www.luminatofestival.com; Jun) Performing-arts and ideas festival featuring some of the world's top creatives.

Toronto Jazz Festival (416-928-2033; www.tojazz.com; late Jun; Michael Franti pictured above) Ten days of jazz, blues and soul, held everywhere from parks to concert halls.

Best Arts & Culture Festivals

Doors Open Toronto (www.toronto.ca/doorsopen; free; late May) Architecturally and historically significant buildings open their doors for public viewing one weekend a year.

International Festival of Authors (416-973-4000; www.readings.org; York Quay, 235 Queens Quay W; from $20; late Oct) Acclaimed writers come for readings, talks, book signings and more.

Nuit Blanche Toronto (http://nbto.com; 1st Sat Oct) One night, all night, of countless urban art experiences around town.

Foodie Festivals Summer

For a showcase of Toronto's culinary diversity, check out the prix fixe food fest of **Summerlicious** (p139) with hundreds of participating restaurants. For a more informal fest, head to **Union Summer** (p53) food market with gourmet food stalls, live music and outdoor film screenings.

Shopping

Shopping in Toronto is a big deal. When it's -20°C outside, you have to fill the gap between brunch and the movies with something, right? People like to update their wardrobes and redecorate their homes, or just walk around the sprawling Eaton Centre. This habit continues through to summer, making boutique-hopping an excuse to hit the streets.

KIEV.VICTOR/SHUTTERSTOCK ©

Best Souvenirs

Spacing Store *Spacing*-magazine gift shop with unique Toronto souvenirs, including ones showcasing particular neighborhoods. (p57)

Outer Layer Well-curated shop selling whimsical gifts and knickknacks from Toronto and Canada beyond. (p57)

Best Markets

St Lawrence Market Complex Classic Toronto market experience since the 1800s. (pictured; p60)

Sunday Antique Market Toronto's best antique market, set in St Lawrence Market Complex. (p61)

Best Art & Artisanal Works

Bay of Spirits Gallery Spectacular gallery showcasing indigenous Canadian art. (p101)

Craft Ontario Shop Longtime gallery-boutique specializing in works by Ontario-based artisans. (p128)

Arts Market Eclectic art collective featuring a unique items made by locals. (p141)

Best Books

Glad Day Oldest operating LGBTIQ+ bookstore on earth. (p88)

Type Books Charming independent bookstore with a top-notch children's-book section. (p128)

Shopping Tips

○ Save your shopping for Thursday and Friday evenings, when stores stay open late.

○ Mom-and-pop shops in Kensington Market and Chinatown often accept cash only.

○ Toronto applies 13% sales tax to all purchases.

Freebies

Despite being one of the priciest cities in Canada, Toronto still has plenty of free or pay-what-you-can offerings for travelers on a budget. That includes historic sights, art and theater, concerts and even tours. In the summer, a bounty of free festivals and outdoor events makes exploring the city as accessible as it is fun.

NATHAN IRWIN/ALAMY STOCK PHOTO ©

Best Free Sights & Tours

Evergreen Brick Works A factory reimagined as a community gathering place and park. (p132)

Riverdale Farm A rural oasis that serves as a working farm and museum. (p138)

Distillery District Victorian warehouses repurposed into boutiques, eateries, galleries and theater spaces. (p65)

Heritage Toronto Local experts lead excellent city tours with historical, cultural and outdoorsy spins. (p110)

Best Free Art

401 Richmond An 18,500-sq-meter artists collective with more than 140 galleries, exhibition spaces, studios and shops. (p50)

Graffiti Alley A back alley off Queen St W featuring 400m of back-to-back murals and street art. (pictured; p50)

Power Plant Contemporary Art Gallery A waterfront gallery featuring one of Toronto's best contemporary-art collections. (p35)

Best Free Performances

Canadian Opera Company Weekly concerts in the opera house's impressive glass-enclosed amphitheater. (p56)

Shakespeare in High Park Open-air performances of the Bard's greatest hits in one of the city's best parks. (p119)

Discount Cards

Toronto CityPASS (www.citypass.com/toronto; adult/child $73/50) offers a bundled rate for five attractions: the CN Tower, Ripley's Aquarium of Canada, the Royal Ontario Museum, Casa Loma and your choice of the Ontario Science Centre or Toronto Zoo. If you're planning to go to at least three of these, it's a good deal.

Plan Your Trip Freebies

For Kids

Toronto is a kid-friendly city with a wide range of options for children of all ages: museums and parks, sights and thrills, even beaches and water play. The city makes it easy for families too – from discounted admission rates to kids-stay-free hotel perks. Add kid menus and restaurants that graciously accommodate picky eaters and you've got a happy little traveler.

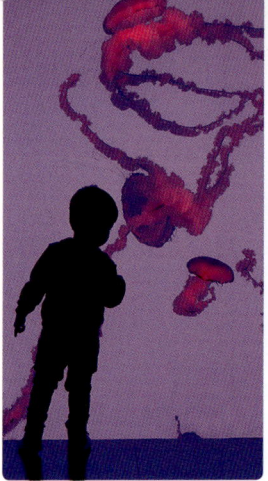

COLIN WOODS/SHUTTERSTOCK ©

Best for Animal Lovers

Ripley's Aquarium of Canada More than 16,000 sea creatures swimming past, around and overhead delight at the aquarium. (pictured; p50)

Riverdale Farm A working urban farm, where children learn about rural life through hands-on fun. (p138)

Spadina Quay Wetlands Explore these wetlands and discover birds, butterflies, turtles...even beavers! (p36)

Best for Creatives

Art Gallery of Ontario Activity stations and a center for DIY art projects keep restless kids happy. (p92)

Harbourfront Centre Watch artists at work – blowing glass, hand-building ceramics, creating textile art. (p30)

Young People's Theatre Catch a play created just for kids. Shows are aimed at different age groups, from under one to over 12s. (p70)

Best for Park- & Beachgoers

High Park Kids enjoy trails, creeks and guided nature walks at this beautiful park. (p118)

Ward's Island Beach A Toronto Islands beach with calm waters and soft tawny sand, perfect for sandcastles. (p41)

Need to Know

Activities Check out www.helpwevegotkids.com for tips on activities, childcare and more.

Transport Kids aged 12 and under ride the TTC for free.

Admission Most sights offer kids free or reduced admission.

LGBTIQ+

To say Toronto is LGBTIQ+ friendly is an understatement. That it embraces diversity more fully than most other cities its size is closer to the mark. In fact, in 2003 Toronto became the first North American city to legalize same-sex marriage. Ground zero of LGBTIQ+ life is the Village, drawing everyone from biker bears to lipstick lesbians to its sunny patios, clubs and cafes.

BOBNOAH/SHUTTERSTOCK ©

Best LGBTIQ+ Nightlife

O'Grady's Irish pub popular for its patio and Dirty Bingo Nights, hosted by drag queens. (pictured; p86)

Crews & Tangos Welcoming bar that doubles as a dance club on weekends. (p87)

Woody's/Sailor Longtime go-to with entertainment and dancing on one side and a sleek bar on the other. (p88)

Glad Day World's oldest gay bookstore, featuring Saturday-night dance parties. (p88)

Best Places to Stay

Anndore House Top choice for style and comfort in the Village. (p148)

Downtown Home Inn Charming B&B with shared bathrooms. (p148)

Victoria's Mansion Inn & Guesthouse Longtime fave of LGBTIQ+ travelers. (p149)

Best LGBTIQ+ Resources

519 (www.the519.org) City agency supporting the LGBTIQ+ community, from recreational classes to counseling.

Canadian Lesbian & Gay Archives (www.clga.ca) Extensive collection of Canadian LGBTIQ+ documentary heritage, open to the public.

Hassle Free Clinic (www.hasslefreeclinic.org) Non-profit providing free sexual health services, including HIV testing.

Queer West (www.queerwest.org) Up-to-date listings of LGBTIQ+ friendly events, bars and restaurants in the Village and West End.

Four Perfect Days

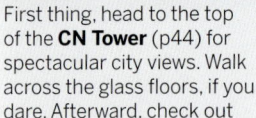

Day 1

First thing, head to the top of the **CN Tower** (p44) for spectacular city views. Walk across the glass floors, if you dare. Afterward, check out **Ripley's Aquarium of Canada** (pictured; p50), where sea creatures swim past visitors in darkened galleries and glass tunnels.

Next, hit **City Hall** (p82) with its clamshell towers and flying-saucer building. Take a photo with the iconic 'Toronto' sign in Nathan Phillips Square.

Walk to Church and Wellesley Sts, the heart of the Village. Pop into gems like **Dead Dog Records** (p89) and **Glad Day** (p88), the world's longest-running gay bookstore. Afterward, play Dirty Bingo at **O'Grady's** (p86), where drag queens call out numbers and hand out risqué prizes.

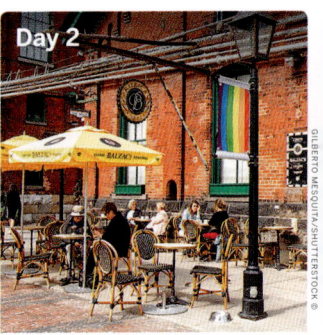

Day 2

Get an early start at the historic **St Lawrence Market** (p60), selling everything from local produce to fresh bread. Nibble your way through it. On weekends, a **Farmers Market** (p61) and **Antique Market** (p61) set up across the street.

Afterward, explore the **Distillery District** (pictured; p65), a set of Victorian-era factories repurposed into boutique shops, restaurants and more.

Take Bus 72 to the **Harbourfront Centre** (p30), a collection of waterfront parks, stages and galleries. Visit **Power Plant Contemporary Art Gallery** (p35), showcasing emerging artists. Cross the plaza to the Harbourfront Centre's **main building** (p30) to see what's playing and to take a spin on the **ice rink** (p36).

Day 3

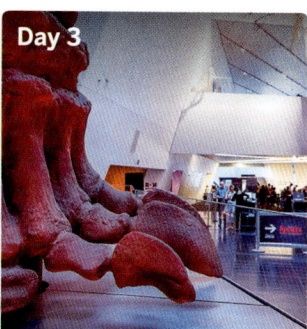

Start at the magnificent **Royal Ontario Museum** (pictured; p104), a massive natural and world history museum. Pick a few sections – Chinese Architecture, First People's Art, Dinosaurs – and call it a morning.

Walk to Kensington Market. Pop into vintage and secondhand stores, keeping an eye out for **Courage My Love** (p100) for clothing and accessories and **Bungalow** (p101) for retro and modern homegoods. Check out the street art – walk down alleys, crane your neck – and consider stopping for a sweet snack at **Dipped Donuts** (p98).

Afterward, catch a set at **Horseshoe Tavern** (p99), an iconic stage for local indie rock, or at **Rex** (p100), an outstanding jazz venue.

Day 4

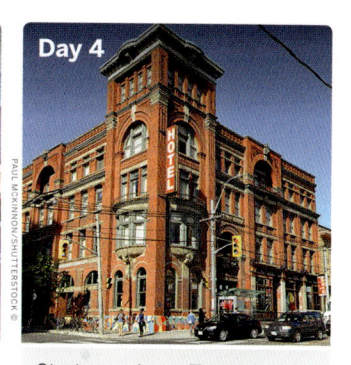

Start your day at **Tommy Thompson Park** (p72), a birder's paradise. Enjoy the sight of water birds, the glittering lake, and downtown Toronto in the distance.

Take Streetcar 501 on Queen St E to the West End, stepping off near Trinity Bellwoods Park. Spend the afternoon window-shopping at hot-ticket shops like **Type Books** (p128) for off-the-beaten-track reads, **House of Vintage** (p128) for designer wear, and **Craft Ontario Shop** (p128) for art by locals.

After dinner at **Julie's Cuban** (p124), walk to **Gladstone Hotel** (pictured; p125) for poetry slams and burlesque or head to **Bar Raval** (p124), a Gaudí-esque spot with strong cocktails and fine wines.

Need to Know
For detailed information, see Survival Guide p147

Currency
Canadian dollar ($)

Time
Eastern Standard Time (GMT/UTC minus four hours)

Languages
English, French

Money
The Canadian dollar ($) is the local currency. ATMs are widely available. Credit cards are accepted in most hotels and restaurants.

Cell Phones
GSM phones typically work in Canada. Arrange for international coverage if you don't already have it.

Tipping
Waitstaff: 15% to 20%
Bartenders: $1 to $2 per drink or 15%, depending on locale
Porters: $2 per bag
Housekeepers: from $5 per day
Taxi drivers: 10% to 15%

Daily Budget

Budget: Less than $100
Dorm bed: $30–50
Double room in a hostel or budget hotel: $100–140
Self-catered meals from markets and supermarkets: $8–14
Subway/streetcar/bus fare: $3.25

Midrange: $100–250
Room in a B&B or midrange hotel: $150–250
Meal at a good local restaurant: from $20 plus drinks
Museum/sight admission: $5–20
Short taxi trip: $10–12

Top end: More than $250
Four-star-hotel room: from $250
Three-course meal at a top restaurant: from $60 plus drinks
Theater tickets: $40–175
Rental car per day: $60–85

Advance Planning

Three months before Buy tickets for a Maple Leafs game or a big-ticket show at the Princess of Wales Theatre.

One month before Book your stay, especially at smaller places such as inns, B&Bs and hostels.

One week before Check out what festivals and events are going on when you'll be in town; make reservations at high-end or happenin' restaurants.

Arriving in Toronto

✈ Toronto Pearson International Airport

Fast rides downtown on UP Express cost $12.35 (kids free); a taxi costs $60.

✈ Billy Bishop Toronto City Airport

Quick access via free ferry and pedestrian tunnel; free shuttle to both from Union Station.

🚌 Union Station

Direct access to subway (Yellow line), streetcars (6, 72B, 121, 509, 510A), GO commuter buses and trains, and VIA long-distance trains.

🚌 Toronto Coach Terminal

Long-distance bus terminal located one block from the Yellow subway line (Dundas).

Getting Around

S Subway

Fastest way across town; 6am (8am Sunday) to 1:30am.

🚗 Streetcar

Extensive service throughout Toronto; 24 hours.

🚌 Bus

Best for areas outside Toronto's core; 6am (8am Sunday) to 1am.

⛴ Boat

Ferries and water taxis provide access to the Toronto Islands.

🚲 Bike

Best for the Waterfront and the Toronto Islands.

🚕 Taxi

Easily hailed downtown. Metered fares from $4.25, plus $1.75 per kilometer.

Union Station

Toronto Neighborhoods

Kensington Market & Chinatown (p91)
A fun, artsy, neighborhood, with used clothing shops, cool little cafes and one of Canada's finest museums – the Art Gallery of Ontario.

West End (p117)
Fun to explore, Toronto's ever-popular West End has diverse eateries, posh shopping and trendy bars. Plus the lovely High Park at the far end.

Entertainment & Financial Districts (p43)
Toronto's bustling downtown has loads of must-sees, including the Hockey Hall of Fame, Graffiti Alley and the ultimate skyscraper – the CN Tower.

Waterfront (p29)
Toronto's long waterfront has sunny pathways, leafy parks, a huge arts complex and even a colonial era fort, all with shimmering views of Lake Ontario.

Yorkville & the Annex (p103)

Busy urban strip with luxury shopping on one end, and cheap eats and university bars on the other. Home to several excellent museums.

Downtown Yonge (p75)

Dense and gritty, and home to terrific destinations like the Elgin and Winter Garden Theatre and the Village, Toronto's spirited gay district.

◉ *Evergreen Brick Works*

◉ *Elgin & Winter Garden Theatre*

◉ *St Lawrence Market Complex*

◉ *Tommy Thompson Park*

◉ *Harbourfront Centre*

◉ *Toronto Islands*

East Toronto & Rosedale (p131)

Once the outskirts of town, East Toronto is popular for its parks and greenways, rich ethnic enclaves, and a fast-rising food and drink scene on Queen Street East.

Old Town, Corktown & Distillery District (p59)

Attractive and walkable, this neighborhood's centuries-old complexes have been reborn as popular gathering spots, filled with bars, galleries, farmers markets and more.

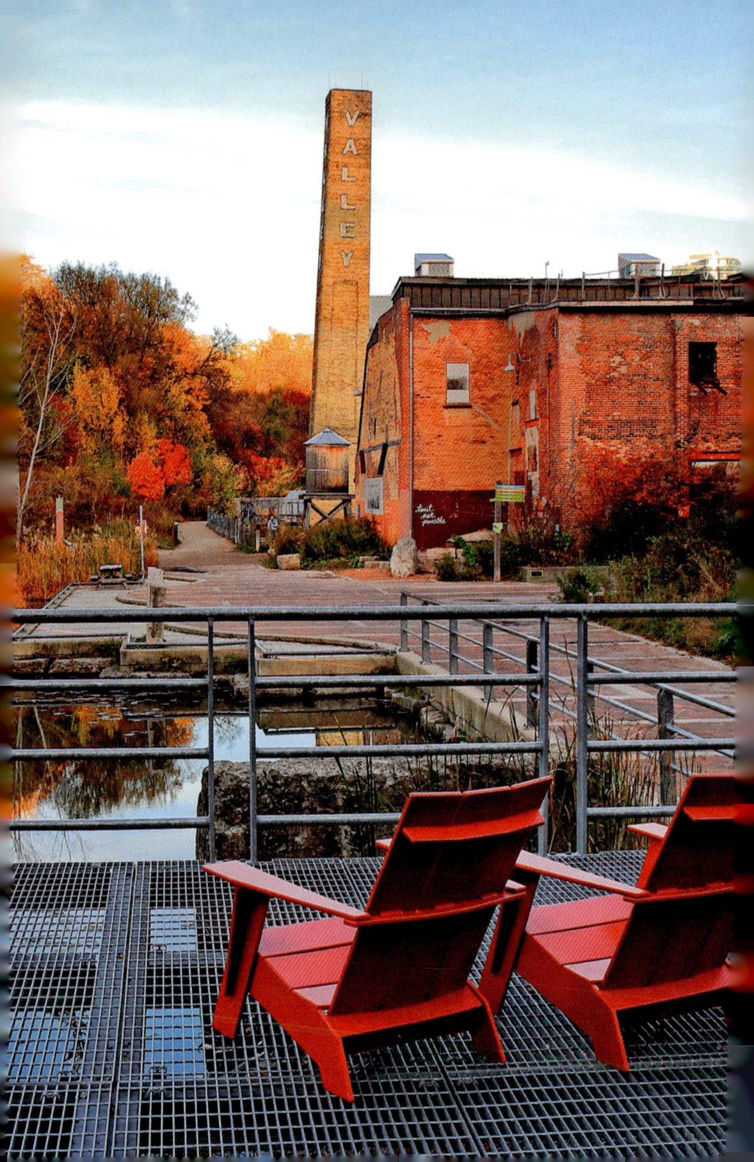
VALLEY

Explore
Toronto

Waterfront	**29**
Entertainment & Financial Districts	**43**
Old Town, Corktown & Distillery District	**59**
Downtown Yonge	**75**
Kensington Market & Chinatown	**91**
Yorkville & the Annex	**103**
West End	**117**
East Toronto & Rosedale	**131**

Worth a Trip

Niagara Falls	142

Toronto's Walking Tours

Along The Lake	32
Architecture & Art	46
Old York Meets New	62
Cabbagetown & City Views	134

Evergreen Brick Works (p132)
CHARLINEXIA ONTARIO CANADA COLLECTION/ALAMY STOCK PHOTO ©

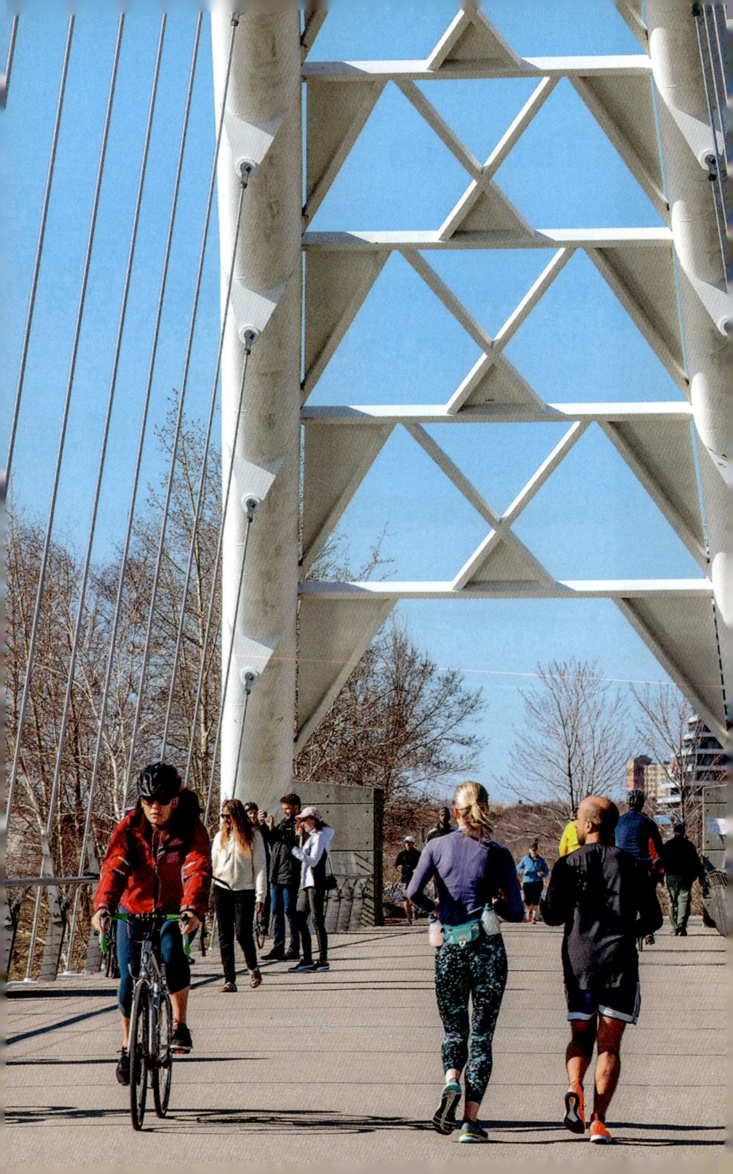

Explore
Waterfront

It's easy to forget, amid Toronto's bustle and chic urbanity, that the city hugs a huge, gorgeous lake. That makes the Waterfront District all the more delightful, with its lakeside parks, art installations, biking and boating. It's all just a few blocks from the CN Tower, yet it remains a locals' secret, mostly due to the relative lack of hotels and well-known restaurants. But the Waterfront is a worthy escape, especially on one of Toronto's bright spring or summer days.

The Short List

- **Harbourfront Centre (p30)** *Exploring galleries, performance venues, boat tours and ice skating, all with beautiful lake views, at this huge outdoor arts and culture complex.*

- **Power Plant Contemporary Art Gallery (p35)** *Recharging your contemporary-art batteries at this popular gallery, with its ever-evolving collection and distinctive painted smokestack.*

- **Fort York National Historic Site (p36)** *Reliving the War of 1812 with tours of the fort's structures as well as live marching and musket demonstrations.*

- **Martin Goodman Trail (p37)** *Biking or strolling along a section of this famous 56km lakefront trail.*

Getting There & Around

Streetcar 509 and 510 run along Queens Quay W, heading to the West Side and neighborhoods to the north.

🚶 Wide sidewalks and a well-maintained trail make the Waterfront very walkable.

🚗 Avoid driving as parking is very limited.

Neighborhood Map on p34

Martin Goodman Trail (p37) through the Humber Bay Arch Bridge
BILL BROOKS/ALAMY STOCK PHOTO ©. HUMBER BAY ARCH BRIDGE ARCHITECTS: MONTGOMERY & SISAM

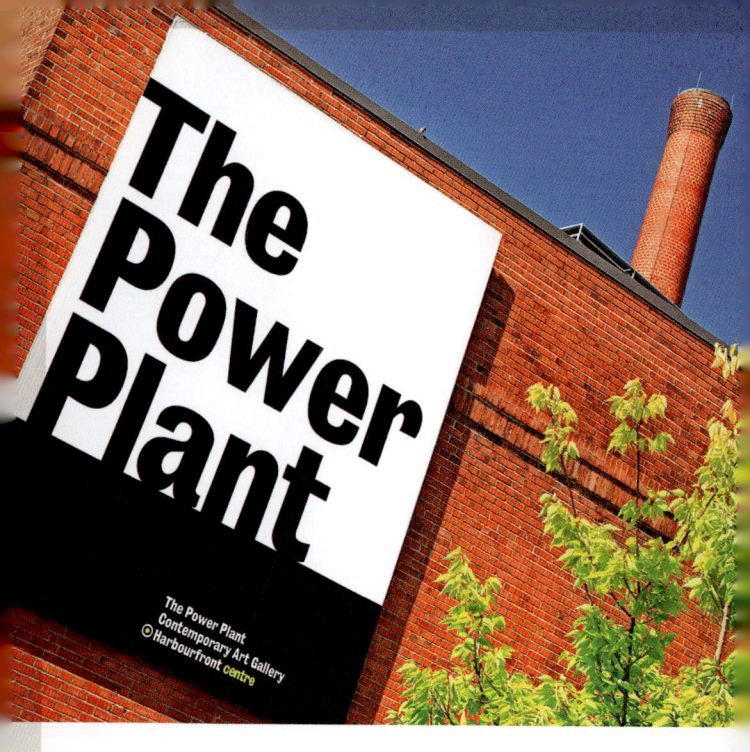

Top Sight
Harbourfront Centre

Practically a neighborhood unto itself, the Harbourfront Centre spreads out over a huge area along the waterfront (4 hectares in all), with an engaging collection of galleries, theaters, places to hang out and paths to stroll down.

- MAP P34, D3
- 416-973-4000
- www.harbourfrontcentre.com
- 235 Queens Quay W
- 10am-11pm Mon-Sat, to 9pm Sun
- P
- 509, 510

Events & Festivals

One of the biggest draws of the Harbourfront Centre is its events and festivals, many of them free. In summer, Thursdays mean **Dancing on the Pier**, which brings live bands and locals in dancing shoes (flip-flops included). In winter the Natrel Rink (p36) becomes a disco with rainbow lights on Saturday nights, with a DJ spinning tunes and folks skating to the beats. Concerts are regularly held in the parks and theaters too.

Power Plant Contemporary Art Gallery

The Power Plant (pictured) is a perfect example of repurposing: a 1926 power plant converted into an airy, two-story art gallery with lake views. Year-round it has rich exhibitions of contemporary work by Canadian and international artists. Above all, the gallery aims to reach a diverse audience, doing so by displaying pieces that address current social issues and by showcasing the work of emerging artists. Free admission ensures that the works, and voices, are accessible to all.

Craft & Design Studios

Wander through the main building of the Harbourfront Centre and you'll encounter open art studios, visible from the outside through glass walls. At this incubator and training center **artists-in-residence** work in five areas: glass, ceramics, design, textiles and jewelry. The public is encouraged to watch and engage with the artists to learn about the art forms. Like what you see? Stop by the on-site **Harbourfront Centre Shop** (416-973-4993; 11am-6pm; 509, 510), which sells works by current and former artists-in-residence.

★ Top Tips

o Renting a bike is fun way to explore the Harbourfront Centre's offerings; with dedicated bike lanes along the waterfront, it's safe, too.

o Adirondack chairs are set up along the waterfront – perfect places to have a picnic lunch with a view.

o Lots of festivals and events are held here year-round. Check the website or stop by the **info desk** to find out what's on.

✕ Take a Break

Don't miss Boxcar Social (p38), a urban-chic cafe in the main building, formerly part of the port complex. It has a terrific patio and lake views to complement its light menu and coffee drinks.

Walking Tour

Along The Lake

Toronto's waterfront district is just south of the downtown area and CN Tower, yet pleasingly removed from the bustle of the city center. Attractions range from the colonial-era Fort York to the delightful Harbourfront Centre, with its industrial chic cafe, modern art museum and boat tour operators. Enjoy the sunshine and cool lake breezes as you walk between sights.

Walk Facts
Start Fort York National Historical Site
End Queens Quay Terminal
Length 3.2km; 3½ hours

❶ Fort York

Start your tour with a bit of history at the **Fort York National Historic Site** (p36), featuring musket displays and docents in period dress. Exiting the fort area, but staying on the Fort York grounds, follow the footpath to **The Bentway**, an innovative park located underneath the elevated Gardiner Expwy. A figure-eight path is used for ice skating in winter and for strolling and art displays the rest of the year.

❷ Martin Goodman Trail

Exit at the eastern end of The Bentway and walk south through **June Callaway Park**, which runs adjacent to Bastion St, to busy Lakeshore Ave. You'll have to walk a block east to the crosswalk to get across the busy street; afterward, continue south on Stadium St, then turn left onto Queens Quay West. This is a section of the **Martin Goodman Trail** (p37), Ontario's famous lakefront pathway.

❸ Toronto Music Garden

Walking east, in a block you'll pass cozy **Little Norway Park**, near the **entrance to the municipal airport** (p149) – oddly enough. Then, a couple blocks further, the **Toronto Music Garden** (p35), with its Bach-inspired landscaping, and **Spadina Quay Wetlands** (p36), are both on a thin wedge of reclaimed greenery between Queens Quay W and the Spadina Quay Marina.

❹ HTO Waterfront Parks

Continuing east, you'll pass the twin **HTO** urban waterfront parks (the name is a play on H2O and TO, for Toronto) and three **Wavedecks** – short, playful undulating boardwalks that replaced ugly sections of retaining wall – at Spadina Ave and Rees and Simcoe Sts.

❺ Harbourfront Centre

Ultimately you'll reach the main building of the **Harbourfront Centre** (p30), the Waterfront's crown jewel. Budget plenty of time to explore this large complex. You can grab a coffee or a bite to eat at **Boxcar Social** (p38), ponder modern artwork at the outstanding **Power Plant Contemporary Art Gallery** (p35), perfect your salchow at the **Natrel Rink** (p36) or book a harbor tour – options range from **kayaking** (p37) to **cruises** (416-203-0178; www.mariposacruises.com; Queens Quay Terminal, 207 Queens Quay W; 45min tours adult/child $26/20; May-Sep; 509, 510).

❻ Queen's Quay Terminal

There's just one more stop after the Harbourfront Centre: **Queen's Quay Terminal** (p39). Built in a repurposed warehouse, and located adjacent to the center, it has a handful of tour operators and eateries on the ground floor.

Waterfront

For reviews see	
◎ Top Sights	p30
◉ Sights	p35
⊗ Eating	p38
◉ Drinking	p39

Sights

Power Plant Contemporary Art Gallery
GALLERY

1 ⊙ MAP P34, D3

Easily recognized by its painted smokestack, the Power Plant gallery is just that: a former power plant transformed into Toronto's premier gallery of contemporary art. Best of all, it's free and exhibitions change regularly. Free kid-centered tours and workshops are offered throughout the month; call to reserve a spot. It's part of the Harbourfront Centre (p30) complex. (☏416-973-4949; www.thepowerplant.org; 231 Queens Quay W; free; ⊙10am-5pm Tue, Wed & Fri-Sun, to 8pm Thu; P ⊙; ☐509, 510)

Toronto Music Garden
GARDENS

2 ⊙ MAP P34, B3

Delicately strung along the western harbor front, the Toronto Music Garden was designed in collaboration with cellist Yo-Yo Ma. It expresses Bach's *Suite No 1 for Unaccompanied Cello* through landscape, with an arc-shaped grove of conifers, a swirling path through a wildflower meadow and a grass-stepped amphitheater where free concerts are held, including **Summer Music in the Garden**, a classical series presented every Thursday (7pm) and Sunday (4pm) from June to September. (☏416-973-4000; www.harbourfrontcentre.com; 479 Queens Quay W; ☐509, 510)

Toronto Music Garden

Spadina Quay Wetlands PARK

3 MAP P34, B3

A former lakeside parking lot has been transformed into the 2800-sq-meter Spadina Quay Wetlands, a thriving, sustainable ecosystem full of frogs, birds, fish and butterflies. When lakeside fishers noticed that northern pike were spawning here each spring, the city took it upon itself to create this new habitat. Complete with flowering heath plants, poplar trees and a birdhouse, it's a little gem that led the way in the harborfront's redevelopment. (416-392-1111; www.toronto.ca; 479 Queens Quay W; dawn-dusk; 509, 510)

Fort York National Historic Site HISTORIC SITE

4 MAP P34, A2

Established by the British in 1793 to defend the then town of York, Fort York was almost entirely destroyed during the War of 1812 when a small band of Ojibwe warriors and British troops were unable to defeat their US attackers. Several structures – barracks, block houses and powder magazines – were immediately rebuilt and still stand on the 17-hectare site. From May to September, men decked out in 19th-century British military uniforms carry out marches and drills, firing musket volleys into the sky. (416-392-6907; www.fortyork.ca; 250 Fort York Blvd; adult/child $14/6; 10am-5pm Jun-Aug, 10am-4pm Mon-Fri, to 5pm Sat & Sun Sep-May; P 509, 511)

Local Experiences

Working out If you're looking for some exercise, skip the hotel gym and go for a jog along the waterfront paths.

Eating Join office workers at **Queen's Quay Terminal** (p39) for a quick or cheap bite.

Working remotely Weekday mornings, **Boxcar Social** (p38) is filled with locals on their laptops.

Sugar Beach Park BEACH

5 MAP P34, F3

Named after the Redpath Sugar Refinery next door, Sugar Beach is a sweet little spot located near Old Toronto. The urban beach park is filled with pastel-pink umbrellas and located by the water, so you can enjoy scenic views and sandy toes. Swimming is prohibited, unfortunately, but a maple-leaf splash pad kinda makes up for it. (www.toronto.ca; 11 Dockside Dr; free; 8am-11pm; 6, 72)

Natrel Rink ICE SKATING

6 MAP P34, D3

A great little ice rink fronting Lake Ontario that's popular with kids and grown-ups alike. Saturday night brings DJ Skate Nights and a party vibe. Skate rentals (adult/child $13/8) are available, including helmets for kids. (416-954-9866; www.harbourfrontcentre.com;

Harbourfront Centre, 235 Queens Quay W; free; 9am-10pm Sun-Thu, to 11pm Fri & Sat Nov-Mar; 509, 510)

Martin Goodman Trail   WALKING

7 MAP P34, C3

The Martin Goodman Trail, a 56km path running the length of Toronto's lakeshore, cuts through the Waterfront neighborhood. The relatively flat path is mostly paved; it's used by joggers, cyclists and folks just out for a stroll. From here, the prettiest direction is east toward the Humber River Bridge, passing urban parks and beaches along the way. (Queens Quay W)

Harbourfront Canoe & Kayak Centre   WATER SPORTS

8 MAP P34, C3

Centrally located, this outfit makes it easy to get on the water, with kayak, canoe and paddleboard rentals. Two- to three-hour guided tours of the Toronto Islands – in either a kayak or a traditional voyageur canoe – are offered, too. (Paddle Toronto; 416-203-2277; https://paddletoronto.com; 283 Queens Quay W; kayaks/canoes/paddleboards for up to 2hr from $45/60/50, tours per person $50-135; noon-8:30pm Mon-Fri, 10am-5:30pm Sat & Sun; 509, 510)

Military re-enactment, Fort York National Historic Site

Tall Ship Kajama
BOATING

9 MAP P34, D3

The dashing 165ft three-masted *Kajama*, a 1930 German trading schooner, sails from the foot of Lower Simcoe St; there's usually a ticket kiosk beside Queens Quay Terminal. Reservations can be made online. (416-203-2322; www.tallshipcruisestoronto.com; 249 Queens Quay W, Suite 111; 90min cruises adult/child $31/17; May-Sep; 509, 510)

Wheel Excitement
CYCLING

10 MAP P34, C3

Close to the ferries for the Toronto Islands; day rentals here are cheaper than hiring on Centre Island and give you the freedom to explore further afield. Options include road bikes, cruisers and hybrids. (416-260-9000; www.wheelexcitement.ca; 249 Queens Quay W; bicycles per hour/day $15/35; 10am-5pm; 509, 510)

Eating

Boxcar Social
CAFE $

11 MAP P34, D3

An industrial-chic cafe/bar/coffee haven, Boxcar Social has enviable views of Lake Ontario. The menu matches the vibe, with fresh takes on salads and sandwiches (kale caesar salad, anyone?). Mornings bring locals with coffee and computers; evenings bring drinks on the patio and twinkling lights. (844-726-9227; www.boxcarsocial.ca; Harbourfront Centre, 235 Queens Quay

Tall Ship Kajama

Canadian National Exhibition

Dating from 1879, '**The Ex**' (CNE; 416-263-3330; www.theex.com; btwn Strachan Ave & Dufferin St; adult/child $20/16; late Aug-early Sep; 509, 511) features more than 700 exhibitors, agricultural shows, lumberjack competitions, outdoor concerts and carnivalia at **Exhibition Place** (416-263-3600; www.explace.on.ca; btwn Strachan Ave & Dufferin St; P; 509, 511), off Lake Shore Blvd W, in the 18 days leading up to Labour Day (the first Monday of September). The air show and Labour Day fireworks take the cake.

W; mains $12-18; 9am-5pm Mon, to 11pm Tue-Thu, to late Fri, 10am-late Sat, to 8pm Sun; 509, 510)

Queen's Quay Terminal FAST FOOD $

12 MAP P34, D3

A big commercial center right on the water with a lots of fast eats and a couple of chain restaurants. There's a small supermarket inside, too, with a great prepared-food section (there's even sushi made to order!). Good if you're looking to get a quick bite or fixins' for a picnic by the water. (207 Queens Quay W; mains from $5; 7am-10pm Mon-Fri, 8am-10pm Sat & Sun; 509, 510)

Harbour 60 STEAK $$$

13 MAP P34, D2

Inside the isolated 1917 Toronto Harbour Commission building, this baroque dining room glows with brass lamps and plush booths. Indulge yourself in a variety of enormous steaks, seasonal Florida stone-crab claws and broiled Caribbean lobster tail. Side dishes are big enough for two. Reservations essential. (416-777-2111; www.harboursixty.com; 60 Harbour St; mains $20-175; 11:30am-2am Mon-Fri, 5pm-2am Sat, to midnight Sun; 509, 510)

Drinking

Against the Grain Urban Tavern PUB

14 MAP P34, F3

The best feature of this yuppyish pub is its enormous lakefront patio (seasonal), with some of the best views of the Toronto harbor front. Come with a friend to enjoy the sunshine and a couple of martinis. If you get hungry, share a plate of sesame-ginger calamari. (647-344-1562; http://fabrestaurants.ca/restaurant/against-the-grain-corusquay; 25 Dockside Dr; 11am-10pm Mon-Thu, to midnight Fri, 10:30am-midnight Sat, to 10pm Sun; 509)

Top Sight
Toronto Islands

There's no better place to admire Toronto's scenic skyline and enjoy a day of leisure than the Toronto Islands. Just 2km offshore, they offer spectacular views back toward the city, several rustic beaches; and waterways for paddling, all accessible via lakeshore bike paths. Best of all, the islands are car-free. Things definitely get jammed in summer; but indie-minded travelers can still find pockets of true getaway.

www.torontoisland bicyclerental.com

Centre Island

per hour bicycles/ tandems $9/16, 2-/4-seat quadricycles $18/32

⏱ 11am-5pm May-Sep

📍 Centre Island

Skyline Views

The skyline views from the Toronto Islands are, without a doubt, some of the best in the city. Pedal to the north side of the islands for the best photo ops. A favorite spot is just east of the Centre Island ferry dock at **Olympic Island**, where a big grassy field, Adirondack chairs and cityscape views invite a leisurely break.

Ward's Island Beach

A short bike ride from the Ward's Island ferry, this like-named beach is long and curving, with tawny sand. The water is calm – there's barely a wave to be had – due to the proximity of Tommy Thompson Park across the water. (In fact, boaters tend to anchor here.) Popular with locals, it's an especially good getaway from the mainland hubbub.

Hanlan's Point Beach

One of the only clothing-optional beaches in all of Canada, Hanlan's Point Beach is a laid-back spot with gorgeous sunset views. Though it's not required, most people bare all. Located at the western end of the Toronto Islands, a bike trail leads straight there.

Paddling Around the Islands

Join a stand-up paddleboard tour with **Toronto Island SUP** (416-899-1668; www.torontoislandsup.com; 13 Algonquin Bridge Rd, Algonquin Island; 2hr tours from $79, yoga $49, rental 1st hour $30, additional hour $10; 10:30am-before sunset Mon-Fri, 10am-6pm Sat & Sun; Ward's Island) to explore the 14 islands of the Toronto Islands archipelago. Morning and afternoon excursions focus on flora and fauna, while night tours let you take in the city views. There are whimsical ukulele tours (yep, paddle and play) and yoga classes on the water, too. Cycle to Algonquin Bridge where SUP boarders launch.

★ Top Tips

- The only bike rental on-island is on Centre Island beach, a short walk from the ferry. It's only open in summer.

- Many people bring bikes from the mainland; rentals are available on the waterfront.

- During low season most shops are closed and restaurants are open on weekends only.

✕ Take a Break

Riviera (416-203-2152; www.islandriviera.com; 102 Lakeshore Ave, Ward's Island; mains $12-17; 11am-11pm; Ward's Island) is a somewhat upscale restaurant with a terrific tree-shaded patio and lake views.

★ Getting There

Ferries to Centre Island and Hanlan's Point (summer only), and Ward's Island (year-round) run from Jack Layton Ferry Terminal frequently and only take 15 minutes.

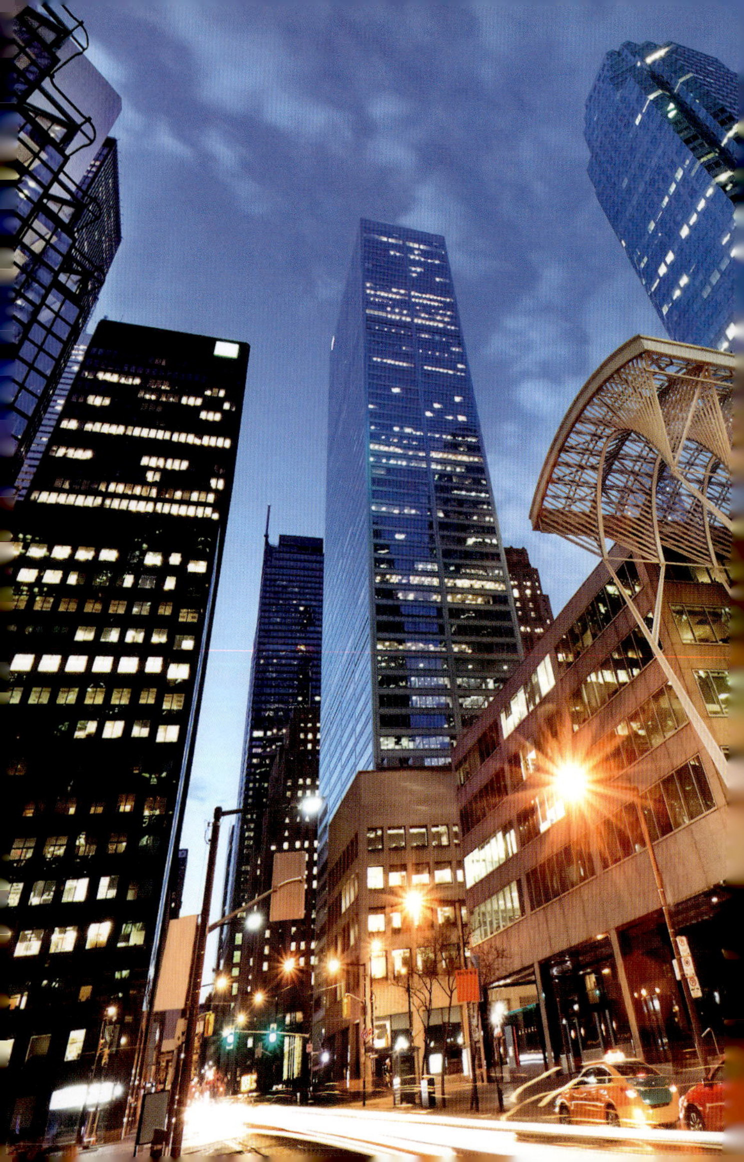

Explore ✦
Entertainment & Financial Districts

The Entertainment and Financial Districts are Toronto's beating heart, home to Canada's 'Wall St,' Union Station (the country's busiest transportation hub) and the city's best-known attractions and nightlife. City sidewalks are ever busy with businesspeople, students, tourists and street performers. It's a logical place for visitors to start, with the CN Tower, Hockey Hall of Fame, theaters, sports and more nearby.

The Short List

- **CN Tower (p44)** *Enjoying awe-inspiring views from the one-time tallest freestanding tower in the world.*

- **Hockey Hall of Fame (p50)** *Practicing your slap shots and admiring the memorabilia at this shrine to Canada's favorite sport.*

- **Performing arts (p56)** *Taking in a big-ticket show at any number of impressive theaters, from uber-modern to turn of the last century.*

- **Spectator sports (p57)** *Joining local fans to cheer on Toronto's high-flying professional sports teams.*

Getting There & Around

[S] The Yellow line has lots of stops downtown that will leave you within a stone's throw of most sights and attractions.

Streetcar Numerous lines converge on downtown, including the 510, heading north–south on Spadina Ave, and east–west routes like the 505 and 506.

Neighborhood Map on p48

Financial District PETER MINTZ/DESIGN PICS/GETTY IMAGES ©

Top Sight
CN Tower

An iconic sight, once the tallest freestanding structure on the planet (553m), the CN Tower is a must-see. Yes, it's expensive. Yes, there are queues. But once you're up there, oohing and aahing over the spectacular city views, looking down 147 stories through glass floors, or even hanging off the outside of the structure, you'll be glad you came.

◎ MAP P48, E5

La Tour CN

☏ 416-868-6937

www.cntower.ca

301 Front St W

Tower Experience adult/child $38/28

⏰ 8:30am-11pm

Ⓢ Union

LookOut-Level Views

A 58-second ride on a glass-fronted elevator leads to perhaps the most spectacular sight in the city: a 360-degree view of Toronto, spread below like a shimmering carpet. Floor-to-ceiling windows make it seem as though you could reach out and touch the skyscrapers. (The windows also make taking photos easier: their darkness adjusts relative to the sunlight.) Come at twilight to see the city transform from day to night, almost magical with its twinkling lights.

Outdoor Sky Terrace Glass Floor

The Outdoor Sky Terrace, 342m high, boasts the CN Tower's original glass floor – the world's first when it was inaugurated in 1994. (There's now another one a level up.) Walking across it, seemingly nothing between your steps and the city streets far below, is surprisingly difficult, even for those with no fear of heights. Don't worry, it won't break – designed to withstand the weight of 35 moose, each floor panel is 6.35cm thick, with four layers of clear tempered glass, plus a layer of air for insulation to keep the room warm.

EdgeWalk

Those with nerves of steel can walk around the 1.5m-wide perimeter of the main pod (pictured), with no windows, no fence, no nothing between you and the city far below. Leaning forward over the tips of your toes is encouraged. (Gulp.) A tether to a metal rail keeps you safe.

★ Top Tips

- Get here before 10am to avoid the longest lines, especially during summer and school vacations. (Or spend a little extra for a timed ride up.)
- Buy your tickets online or using the CN Tower app to save 15%.
- Skip the SkyPod observation deck – it can become cramped and stuffy, and really isn't worth the extra cost.
- Stay awhile! Buy a drink and settle in with a book or a deck of cards. With no fixed length of stay and plenty of seating, why not?

✕ Take a Break

- On the LookOut observation level, **VUE Bistros** sells pastries and baked goods, plus hot and cold drinks, with floor-to-ceiling window views.
- 360° restaurant has upscale lunch and dinner service on a revolving platform.

Walking Tour

Architecture & Art

The Entertainment and Financial Districts have some of Toronto's most iconic and popular destinations – namely, the CN Tower and Hockey Hall of Fame. But take a stroll along the busy downtown streets, and you'll encounter museums, pocket parks, and some striking artwork and architecture. Time permitting, catch a concert or even a Blue Jays ball game.

Walk Facts

Start Union Station
End Steam Whistle Brewing
Length 2.8km; 2½ hours

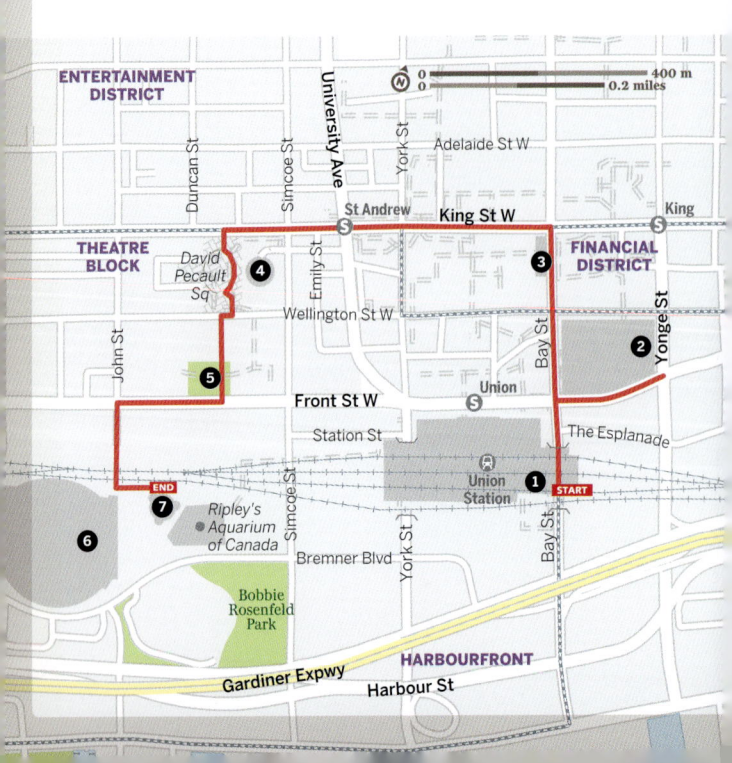

❶ Union Station

Start at **Union Station** (📞416-869-3000; https://torontounion.ca; 140 Bay St; Ⓢ Union, 🚋509, 510), Toronto's main transportation hub and Canada's largest train station. Admire its 22 columns, each 12m tall and weighing 75 tons, before heading into the Great Hall with its vaulted ceiling and provincial flags. Meander through the building, exiting via the southernmost door at Bay St.

❷ Hockey Hall of Fame

Turn left, walking through the tunnel, past the **mural of notable indigenous Canadians**. Take a right at Front St. A block later is the rococo facade of the **Hockey Hall of Fame** (p50), once the Bank of Montreal building but now attached to what's called the Crystal Cathedral, a massive, glass-enclosed commercial center.

❸ Design Exchange

Return to Bay St, turn right and you'll see the **Design Exchange** (p51), a tiny design museum housed in what was the Toronto Stock Exchange. Admire the gleaming art deco doors. Head to King St and take a left. Steps away, a small park holds '**The Pasture**,' Joe Fafard's collection of life-size bronze cows in repose, a stark contrast to the skyscrapers above.

❹ Roy Thomson Hall & Pecault Square

Continue on King St to **Roy Thomson Hall**, the Jello-mold-shaped building, home to the **Toronto Symphony Orchestra** (p56). Wander through adjacent **David Pecault Square**, an urban space with stone benches and, on weekdays, pop-up eateries.

❺ Simcoe Park

Cross Wellington St to **Simcoe Park** and Anish Kapoor's striking '**Mountain**' sculpture, with the CN Tower looming in the background.

❻ Rogers Centre

Cross Front St and take the pedestrian bridge over the train tracks. The **Rogers Centre** (p51), home of the Blue Jays, is on the right, the CN Tower on the left. As you walk, admire '**The Audience**,' a baseball-themed frieze by Michael Snow.

❼ CN Tower and Ripley's Aquarium

At the end of the bridge, turn left toward the **CN Tower** (p44) and **Ripley's Aquarium of Canada** (p50). Find the perfect angle to take some selfies with the 553m tower looming above you. Consider heading to the top to enjoy the view.

Entertainment & Financial Districts

Entertainment & Financial Districts

Map Legend — For reviews see
- Top Sights — p44
- Sights — p50
- Eating — p51
- Drinking — p54
- Entertainment — p55
- Shopping — p57

Key locations labeled on map:
- CN Tower (2)
- Ripley's Aquarium of Canada
- Hockey Hall of Fame (1)
- Design Exchange (5)
- Union Station
- Ontario Travel Information Centre
- Metro Convention Centre
- David Pecaulat Sq
- Simcoe Park
- Bobbie Rosenfeld Park
- Theatre Block
- Entertainment District
- Financial District
- Harbourfront

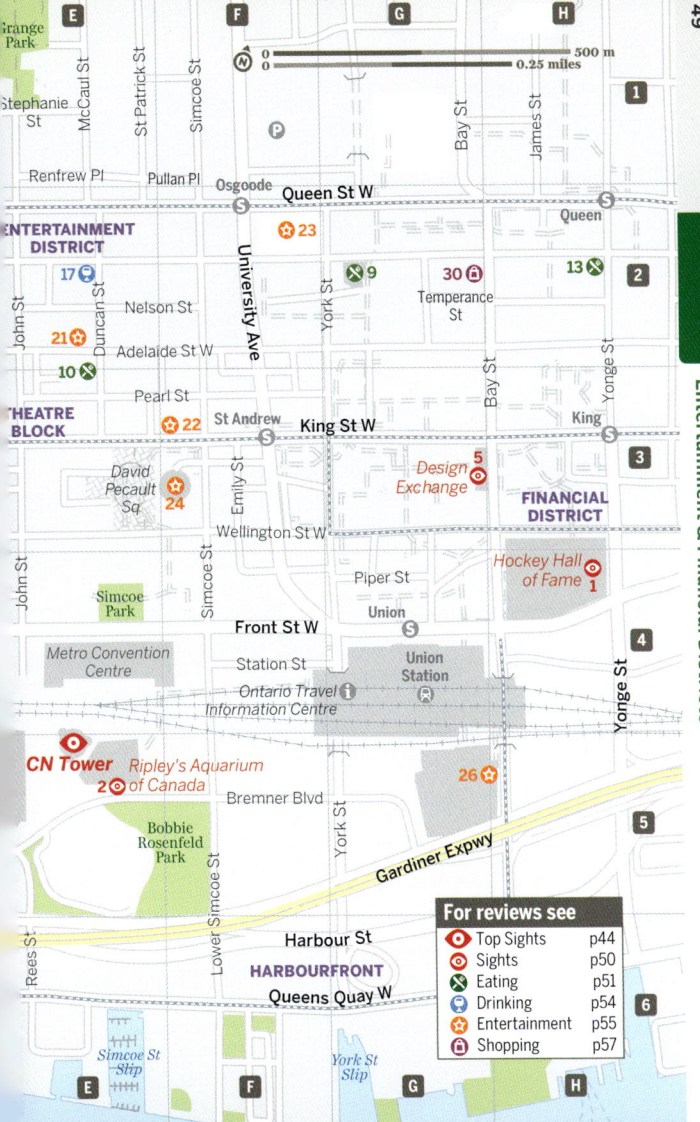

Streets: Queen St W, Osgoode, Renfrew Pl, Pullan Pl, Nelson St, Adelaide St W, Pearl St, King St W, Wellington St W, Piper St, Front St W, Station St, Bremner Blvd, Gardiner Expwy, Harbour St, Queens Quay W, University Ave, York St, Bay St, Yonge St, James St, Temperance St, Emily St, John St, Duncan St, Simcoe St, Lower Simcoe St, Rees St, McCaul St, St Patrick St, Stephanie St

Numbered points: 9, 10, 13, 17, 21, 22, 23, 24, 26, 30

Scale: 500 m / 0.25 miles

Sights

Hockey Hall of Fame MUSEUM

1 MAP P48, H4

Inside the rococo gray-stone Bank of Montreal building (c 1885), the Hockey Hall of Fame is a Canadian institution. Even those unfamiliar with the rough, super-fast sport are likely to be impressed by this, the world's largest collection of hockey memorabilia. Check out the *Texas Chainsaw Massacre*–like goalkeeping masks or go head to head with the great Wayne Gretzky, virtual-reality style. And, of course, be sure to take a pic with the beloved Stanley Cup. (416-360-7765; www.hhof.com; Brookfield Place, 30 Yonge St; adult/child $20/14; 9:30am-6pm Mon-Sat, 10am-6pm Sun Jun-Sep, 10am-5pm Mon-Fri, 9:30am-6pm Sat, 10:30am-5pm Sun Oct-May; S Union)

Ripley's Aquarium of Canada AQUARIUM

2 MAP P48, E5

Arguably one of Toronto's best attractions for both young and old, with more than 16,000 aquatic animals and 5.7 million liters of water in the combined tanks. There are touch tanks, a glass tunnel with a moving walkway, educational dive presentations…and even live jazz on the second Friday of each month. Open 365 days a year. Peak hours are 11am to 4pm. (647-351-3474; www.ripleysaquariumofcanada.com; 288 Bremner Blvd; adult/child $32/22; 9am-11pm; S Union)

401 Richmond GALLERY

3 MAP P48, C2

Inside an early-20th-century lithographer's warehouse, restored in 1994, this 18,500-sq-meter New York–style artists collective hums with the creative vibes of more than 140 contemporary galleries, exhibition spaces, studios and shops representing works in almost any medium you can think of. Speaker series and film fests are held throughout the year. Grab a snack at the ground-floor cafe (open 9am to 5pm Monday to Friday) and enjoy it on the expansive roof garden, a little-known oasis in summer. (416-595-5900; www.401richmond.com; 401 Richmond St W; free; 9am-7pm Mon-Fri, to 6pm Sat; 510)

Graffiti Alley PUBLIC ART

4 MAP P48, B2

Possibly the most popular place to check out street art in Toronto (and there are many), this back alley has a magnificent collection of colorful murals and street art. Spanning three blocks (about 400m), the alley was popularized as the location of Rick Mercer's rants on CBC comedy program the *Rick Mercer Report*. Great for photo ops. (Rush Lane; Graffiti Alley, btwn Spadina Ave & Portland St; 301, 501)

Design Exchange
MUSEUM

5 MAP P48, G3

The original Toronto Stock Exchange now houses eye-catching industrial-design exhibits. The permanent collection of this rather tiny museum includes more than 1000 Canadian pieces that span six decades. There are free one-hour tours the last Friday of each month, starting at noon. (DX; 416-363-6121; www.dx.org; 234 Bay St; free; 9am-5pm Tue-Fri, noon-4:30pm Sat; S King)

Rogers Centre
STADIUM

6 MAP P48, D5

Technically awe-inspiring, the Rogers Centre opened in 1989 with the world's first fully retractable dome roof and seating for up to 53,500 people. Tours include a brain-scrambling video wall screening footage of past sporting glories, concerts and events; a sprint through a box suite; a locker-room detour (sans athletes); and a memorabilia museum. A budget seat at a **Blue Jays** (www.bluejays.com) baseball game is the cheapest way to see the center. (416-341-2770; 1 Blue Jays Way; 1hr tours adult/child $17/10; S Union)

Eating

Ravi Soups
INTERNATIONAL $

7 MAP P48, D2

This one's pretty simple: a small menu of seven soups (the likes of corn chowder with blue crab or porcini-mushroom wild-rice bisque), five wraps (eg curried

Ripley's Aquarium of Canada

lamb with roasted yams) and four salads (eg baby spinach with mango-pineapple salsa) that are done to perfection. There's a small eating area with a long shared table and a small patio with psychedelic art. (☎647-435-8365; www.ravisoup.com; 322 Adelaide St W; soups $10.99; ⏱11am-10pm; 🚋504, 508)

Wilbur Mexicana   MEXICAN $

8 MAP P48, B3

This is Mexican street-food heaven, from the industrial-chic atmosphere to the standout Baja fish tacos. Complete with a fully stocked apothecary cabinet filled with salsas and hot sauces, this hip little taco joint pays homage to Wilbur Scoville, founder of the Scoville scale, which measures the spiciness of chilies. (☎416-792-1878; http://wilburmexicana.com; 552 King St W; tacos $4-5, mains $11-15; ⏱11:30am-10pm Mon-Sat, noon-9pm Sun; 🚋504)

Assembly Chef's Hall   FOOD HALL $$

9 MAP P48, G2

Home to a diverse set of global cuisines by some of Toronto's top chefs, this is less food court and more sprawling upscale eatery. There's everything from margherita pizza to pork *carnitas* tacos and *khao soi* beef. Weekday lunch hours are crowded with suits and professional attire (it's in the heart of the Financial District), but

Hotbunzz Street Cuisine, Union Summer

dinnertime is much more chill and relaxed. (☎647-557-5993; www.assemblychefshall.com; 111 Richmond St E; mains $12-19; ⏱7am-10pm Mon-Fri, 10am-10pm Sat; 🚇Osgoode)

Pai   THAI $$

10 MAP P48, E3

Pai is known for its spectacular food and lively ambience, so you'll pretty much always see lines out the door no matter the time of day. The *khao soi* (curry noodle soup) is what you might see all over social media; it's definitely one of the best Thai dishes you'll find in town. (☎416-901-4724; www.paitoronto.com; 18 Duncan St; mains $14-18; ⏱11:30am-10pm Mon-Thu, to 10:30pm Fri & Sat, 3-10pm Sun; 🚇St Andrew)

Buca
ITALIC ***

11 MAP P48, A3

A breathtaking basement-level restaurant with exposed-brick walls and a soaring ceiling, Buca serves artisanal Italian fare such as homemade pasta and nose-to-tail-style dishes such as *orecchio di maiale* (crispy pigs' ears) and *cervello* (lamb's brains wrapped in prosciutto and sage). Ease into the experience with a charcuterie board of house-cured meats, flavorful cheeses and bread knots. (416-865-1600; www.buca.ca; 604 King St W; mains $17-55; 11am-3pm & 5-10pm Mon-Wed, 11am-3pm & 5-11pm Thu & Fri, 5-11pm Sat, 5-10pm Sun; 304, 504)

Lee
ASIAN $$$

12 MAP P48, A3

Truly a feast for the senses, dinner at acclaimed *cuisinier* Susur Lee's self-titled flagship is an experience best shared. Slick servers assist in navigating the artisanal selection of East-meets-West delights: you really want to get the pairings right. It's impossible to adequately convey the dance of flavors, textures and aromas one experiences in the signature Singaporean slaw, with...how many ingredients?! (416-504-7867; www.susur.com/lee; 601 King St W; mains $16-38; 5-10:30pm Sun-Wed, to 11pm Thu, to 11:30pm Fri & Sat; 504, 508)

Union Summer

Union Station's summer food market – **Union Summer** (416-338-0889; http://torontounion.ca; Union Station, 65 Front St W; 11am-9pm Mon-Wed, to 10pm Thu-Sat, to 6pm Sun; Union) – has become a fixture in Toronto, with a daily market of gourmet food stalls, activities, free outdoor film screenings, live music and drinks from late May to early August.

Richmond Station
INTERNATIONAL $$$

13 MAP P48, H2

Reservations are strongly advised at this busy and uncomplicated restaurant, brainchild of celebrity *Top Chef Canada* winner Carl Heinrich. Dishes are 'ingredient focused and technique driven.' Try a delicious charcuterie board and buttery lobster spaghetti. The eclectic menu is simple but gratifying, priced right and complemented by a well-paired wine list and daily chalkboard specials. Highly recommended. (647-748-1444; www.richmondstation.ca; 1 Richmond St W; mains $23-32; 11:30am-10:30pm; Queen)

Local Experiences

Hanging out
The swanky rooftop lounge at the **Thompson Toronto** (Map p48, A3; 416-640-7778; www.thompsonhotels.com/toronto; 550 Wellington St W; P ❄ ☎ ☒ ☒ ; ☐ 504, 508) is a go-to for locals year-round – martinis, couches and skyline views; what could top that? During the **Toronto International Film Festival** (p114), celebrities often join in the fun.

Shopping
Sure, souvenir gifts are at all the major downtown sights. But consider heading west to places like **Outer Layer** (p57) and **Spacing Store** (p57), where locals shop for more imaginative gifts and mementos.

Navigation
Head underground: use the city's PATH tunnels to get from place to place and avoid the cold or the traffic.

Forno Cultura   BAKERY

14   MAP P48, A3

An Italian bakery tucked into a basement-level shop, Forno Cultura offers a full line of bread and pastries made with ingredients imported from Italy – even the flour and butter! The bakery itself is a long room, one side lined with impossible-to-resist goods, the other a view of bakers doing their thing. Communal tables encourage you to stay, watch and eat. (416-603-8305; www.fornocultura.com; 609 King St W; items from $3; 7:30am-9:30pm Tue-Sat, 8am-6pm Sun; ☐ 504, 508)

Drinking

Jimmy's   COFFEE

15   MAP P48, A3

Located in a bohemian-chic row house, this hopping coffee joint serves up flavorful coffee drinks – even nitro cold brew on tap – made from beans roasted in-house. Explore and find a cozy spot: upstairs, downstairs, front patio or back, there are lots of options here. If there's a long line, try the original Jimmy's across the street; same coffee, different vibe. (647-347-5600; www.jimmyscoffee.ca; 100 Portland St; 8am-8pm Sun-Thu, to 9pm Fri & Sat;)

Petty Cash
BAR

16 MAP P48, A2

This King West hangout is a millennial's favorite known for its killer cocktails and comfort food. Edgy murals and neon signs make it easy to prove you had a good time with an Instagram photo or two. (647-748-2274; http://pettycashtoronto.com; 487 Adelaide St W; 5pm-2am Mon-Fri, 4pm-2am Sat & Sun; 504)

Fifth Social Club
CLUB

17 MAP P48, E2

Known by regulars as Easy, this upscale club hosts an early to mid-20s crowd. From the chocolate-fondue station to the life-size Jenga and the swing in the middle of the dance floor, this is not your ordinary spot for a weekend outing, but if you're looking to dress up and dance the night away, it's perfect. (416-979-3000; http://fifthsocialclub.thefifth.com; 225 Richmond St W; cover $20-25; 9pm-2:30am Fri, 10pm-2:30am Sat; S Osgoode)

Underground Garage
BAR

18 MAP P48, D3

Trying valiantly to keep it real in a grungy sort of way, this urban rock bar is down a steep staircase lined with Led Zeppelin, Willie Nelson and John Lennon posters. Once inside, it's all about wailing guitars, cold beer and good times (and loads of Christmas lights). In summer, head to the rooftop patio – same vibe with spectacular views. (416-688-8787; www.undergroundgarage.ca; 365 King St W; cover $8-20; 10pm-2am Sun-Wed, 9pm-2am Thu-Sat; 504, 510)

Entertainment

TIFF Bell Lightbox
CINEMA

19 MAP P48, D3

Headquarters of the Toronto International Film Festival (p114), this resplendent cinema complex is the hub of all the action when the festival's in town. Throughout the year it's used primarily for TIFF Cinematheque, screening world cinema, independent films, directorial retrospectives and other special events. Try to see a film here if you can. (888-599-8433; www.tiff.net; 350 King St W; 504)

Second City Toronto
COMEDY

20 MAP P48, D3

Running for decades, Second City has nightly improv and sketch-comedy shows that'll have you laughing all night long. Big-name comedians such as Catherine O'Hara and Mike Myers got their start here. Its training center, the **John Candy Box Theatre**, presents shows by students and budding comics with prices to match; the entrance is around the corner on Blue Jays Way. (416-343-0011; www.secondcity.com/shows/toronto; 51 Mercer St; tickets $28-52, training-center tickets $5-15; S St Andrews, 504)

Adelaide Hall
CONCERT VENUE

21 ⭐ MAP P48, E2

One of the best small venues in town – its acoustics are tops – Adelaide Hall attracts both big-name and up-and-coming acts. On other nights, DJs and cover bands keep the place hopping. Look for the entrance tucked into an alley off Adelaide St (or just follow the line of people). (✆647-344-1234; https://adelaidehallto.com; 250 Adelaide St W; 🚌141, 143, 144, 145)

Royal Alexandra Theatre
THEATER

22 ⭐ MAP P48, F3

The 'Royal Alex,' as she is sometimes affectionately known, is one of the more impressive theaters in the city and home to splashy Broadway musicals. Built in 1907, it's among the oldest continuously operating theaters in Canada, its stage graced by some of the most talented 20th-century artists, including Orson Welles, Fred and Adele Astaire and Edith Piaf. (✆416-872-1212; www.mirvish.com; 260 King St W; Ⓢ St Andrew, 🚋504)

Canadian Opera Company
OPERA

23 ⭐ MAP P48, F2

Canada's national opera company has been warbling its phenomenal pipes for over 50 years. Tickets sell out fast, though standing-room-only tickets are available on performance days. Free concerts in the impressive glass-enclosed Richard Bradshaw Amphitheatre are held from September through May, usually at noon. (✆416-363-8231; www.coc.ca; Four Seasons Centre for the Performing Arts, 145 Queen St W; ⏰box office 11am-7pm Mon-Sat, to 3pm Sun; Ⓢ Osgoode)

Toronto Symphony Orchestra
CLASSICAL MUSIC

24 ⭐ MAP P48, F3

A range of classics, Cole Porter–era pops and new music from around the world are presented by the TSO at Jello-mold-like Roy Thomson Hall (sometimes also at Massey Hall and the Meridian Arts Centre). Reduced ticket prices available (from $19) for music-lovers aged 15 to 35, too. (TSO; ✆416-593-1285; www.tso.ca; Roy Thomson Hall, 60 Simcoe St; ⏰box office 10am-5pm Mon-Fri, noon-5pm Sat; Ⓢ St Andrew)

Factory Theatre
THEATER

25 ⭐ MAP P48, A2

This innovative theater company – 'Home of the Canadian Playwright' – has been busy since 1970 producing exclusively Canadian plays. Stay for the talk backs ('Matt's Chats') with cast members after most shows. Sunday matinees are 'Pay What You Can.' (✆416-504-9971; www.factorytheatre.ca; 125 Bathurst St; tickets from $25; 🚋501, 504A, 504B)

Discounted Show Tickets

Performing-arts tickets aren't cheap in this town, often running $100 or more. Save a few loonies by trying for rush tickets, sold on performance day. For those aged under 30, many venues offer discounted tickets costing just $25.

Scotiabank Arena SPECTATOR SPORT

26 MAP P48, G5

The Scotiabank Arena is home to the 13-time Stanley Cup–winning **Toronto Maple Leafs** (www.mapleleafs.com) and the **Toronto Raptors** (www.nba.com/raptors), the only Canadian team in the NBA. It also hosts countless concerts and big-ticket events. (416-815-5500; www.scotiabankarena.com; 40 Bay St; S Union)

Shopping

Spacing Store GIFTS & SOUVENIRS

27 MAP P48, D2

Spacing is a magazine with a thing for Canadian cities. Its store is a celebration of urban living, with T-shirts, vintage TTC posters and other gifts by local designers. Proudly wear your favorite neighborhood as a button and get the inside staff gossip about upcoming changes to Toronto's streets. (416-644-1017; http://spacing.ca/toronto; 401 Richmond St W; 11am-7pm Mon-Fri, noon-6pm Sat; S Osgoode)

Outer Layer GIFTS & SOUVENIRS

28 MAP P48, B2

A little gift shop selling whimsical and laugh-out-loud knickknacks, accessories and greeting cards, many with a Torontonian or Canadian spin. It's amazingly well curated – few lame ducks here. (416-869-9889; https://outerlayer.com; 577 Queen St W; 11am-7pm Mon-Wed & Sat, to 8pm Thu & Fri, noon-6pm Sun; 301, 501)

Freshly Baked Tees CLOTHING

29 MAP P48, B2

DIY souvenir T-shirt: bring your own text and graphics or have the cool cats behind the desk do it. Ready in five minutes. High-quality cotton T-shirts start at $29. Discounts available for orders of four or more. (416-907-3575; 557 Queen St W; noon-7pm; 301, 501)

Ben McNally BOOKS

30 MAP P48, G2

An independent bookstore owned and run by friendly bookworms, Ben McNally has a wide, interesting selection of titles often not found elsewhere. Book talks and readings are regularly held; check the website for the schedule. (416-361-0032; https://benmcnallybooks.com; 366 Bay St; 9am-6pm Mon-Fri, 11am-5pm Sat; 141, 142, 143, 144, 145)

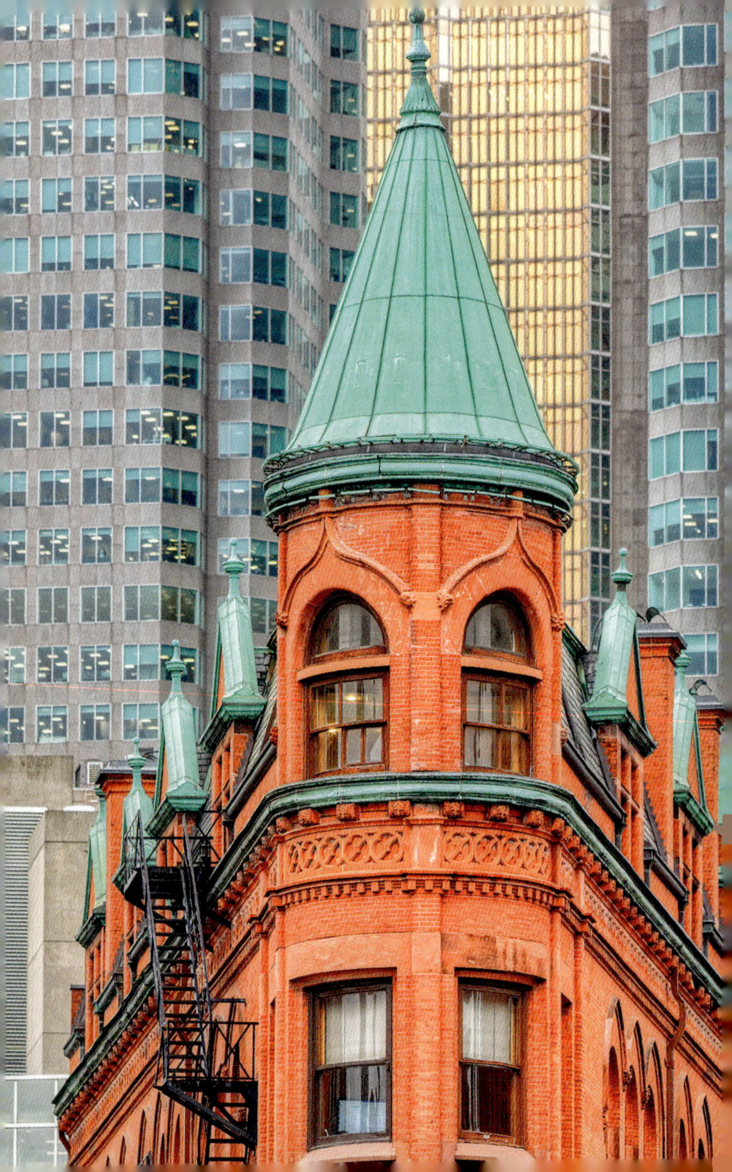

Explore
Old Town, Corktown & Distillery District

This centuries-old part of town has beautifully restored buildings and cobblestone sidewalks, providing a snapshot of Toronto's history. Inside, modern-day fancies take over – bars, upscale eateries, boutique shops and performing-arts spaces. Wander the streets and explore. The ghosts of Toronto's past are here, but the neighborhood is very much alive.

The Short List

- **St Lawrence Market Complex (p60)** Perusing fruits, meats and cheeses, plus antiques, curios and even a museum, at this lively marketplace.
- **Distillery District (p65)** Exploring this converted 19th-century distillery, home to a rich array of shops, restaurants and galleries.
- **Reservoir Lounge (p69)** Listening to jazz, blues and swing in an iconic underground joint.
- **Chef's House (p67)** Enjoying a gourmet meal on a food-court budget, prepared by culinary students.

Getting There & Around

S The yellow line stops near St Lawrence Market at Union Station and King St (at Yonge St).

Streetcar The 503 or 504 streetcars run along King St, from the Entertainment & Financial Districts and the East Side.

Route 121 serves the neighborhood from the Waterfront and Entertainment & Financial Districts.

Neighborhood Map on p64

Flatiron Building (p65) COLIN WOODS/SHUTTERSTOCK ©

Top Sight 📷
St Lawrence Market Complex

A marketplace for over 150 years, the St Lawrence complex is alive with hustle and bustle: food stalls and specialty shops, antique and farmers markets, and the well-restored meeting place St Lawrence Hall, its copper clock tower visible from blocks away. It's a place to explore and enjoy; a place to imagine what life was once like here.

◎ MAP P64, B3

📞 416-392-7219

www.stlawrencemarket.com

92-95 Front St E

🕗 8am-6pm Tue-Thu, to 7pm Fri, 5am-5pm Sat

🅿

🚍 503, 504

Saturday Farmers Market

A cornucopia of colors and flavors greets you at the St Lawrence farmers market. Held every Saturday, it's a bustling affair, bringing locals in to buy fresh produce, artisanal foods and flowers from around the region. Come early – it opens at 5am – for the best of the lot and great photo ops, too. In summer the market spills onto the surrounding streets.

Sunday Antique Market

Over 90 vendors, some from as far as Québec, come to sell their treasures every Sunday at the St Lawrence antique market (pictured). It's an experience: rows and rows of stands filled with everything from books and tableware to jewelry and chandeliers. Considered the best antique market in the city, this is the place to come for a special find or even just a quirky bauble.

Market Kitchen

Located on the mezzanine level of St Lawrence Market South, this 'kitchen' serves as a culinary workshop and event space. One-off classes often include shopping in the market below, meeting vendors and cooking up a feast under the guidance of a professional chef. Others include simply watching the chef prepare a gourmet meal and enjoying it on-site. Either way, it's a win. Ontario wines and craft beers are typically paired with the menus.

Market Gallery

The Market Gallery is a tiny museum with rotating exhibits of paintings, photographs, documents and historical relics of Toronto. It's located at St Lawrence Market South in what was the council chamber – all that remains of Toronto's first City Hall, which stood here from 1845 to 1899. Open Tuesday to Saturday; admission is $8/5 adult/child.

★ Top Tips

- Browse, sample and snack at several food stalls instead of having a full meal at one place.
- You'll get the best produce if you arrive first thing in the morning for the Saturday farmers market.
- Take a cooking class or book a special dinner at the Market Kitchen.

✕ Take a Break

For gourmet dining at St Lawrence Market prices, try Chef's House (p67), where culinary students whip up prix-fixe two-, three- and four-course meals.

Head to the 1950s-style Patrician Grill (p66) for irresistible (and belt-busting) eats such as triple-decker sandwiches and chocolate milkshakes.

Walking Tour 🥾

Old York Meets New

Old meets new in this unique district. Structures that date from the city's founding and industrial hey day also serve as popular destinations for locals and tourists alike. Check out the historic Flatiron Building, adorned with a striking modern mural, and then peruse the farmers market at St Lawrence Market or window-shop in the Distillery District.

Walk Facts

Start Flatiron Building
End Mill Street Brewery
Length 2.7km; three hours

❶ Flatiron Building

Begin at the **Flatiron Building** (p65), the 1892 Gooderham and Worts Distillery headquarters, so named because of its triangular shape. Admire its copper roof and turret as you walk around it, not missing the whimsical **mural** that makes it seem that a curtain of windows is falling off. Head east on Front St. About a block away, stop and turn around for an iconic view: the Flatiron Building perfectly framed by Toronto's skyscrapers.

❷ St Lawrence Market South

Continue east on Front to **St Lawrence Market South** (p60), built in 1845 to serve as Toronto's City Hall. Inside you'll find more than 120 vendors, selling everything from pork belly to raw honey. Wander and graze, taking in the sights and tastes, and check out the **Market Gallery**, with historical exhibits on the city.

❸ Farmers & Antique Markets

Afterward, return to Front St, taking an immediate right down Jarvis St to The Esplanade. On the corner is a huge semi-permanent tent, the temporary home of the **Saturday farmers market** and **Sunday antique market** while the North Market building is reconstructed. Inside, wander past rows upon rows of fresh local produce or, alternatively, antique furniture, tableware and knickknacks.

❹ St Lawrence Hall

Return to Jarvis St, heading north to King St, where **St Lawrence Hall** (p60) sits. A 19th-century meeting place with an impressive copper clock tower, this was where abolitionists campaigned to end slavery in Canada.

❺ Along the Way

Turn right onto King, walking several blocks to Trinity St, along the way poking your head into the **Patrician Grill** (p66) to admire its immaculately preserved 1950s-style diner (if the meat-loaf special is available, be sure to stay and enjoy!). At Trinity St, take a right and continue to Mill St, the heart of the **Distillery District** (p65).

❻ Distillery District

Once the site of the British Empire's largest whiskey distillery, today it's a pedestrian-only area (p65) with cobblestone streets, its factories repurposed into boutiques, galleries, art studios, restaurants and bars. Pop into locally owned **Hoi Bo** (p70) or **Corktown Designs** (p71), or see what's on at the **Young Centre for the Performing Arts** (416-866-8666; www.youngcentre.ca; 50 Tank House Lane; 72, 503, 504). Top off your long walk with a flight at the **Mill Street Brewery** (p68).

Old Town, Corktown & Distillery District

For reviews see
- Top Sights — p60
- Sights — p65
- Eating — p66
- Drinking — p68
- Entertainment — p69
- Shopping — p70

Sights

Distillery District — AREA

1 ◎ MAP P64, F4

Centered on the 1832 Gooderham and Worts distillery – once the British Empire's largest – the 5-hectare Distillery District is one of Toronto's best downtown attractions. Its Victorian industrial warehouses have been converted into soaring galleries, artists studios, design boutiques, cafes and eateries. On weekends, newlyweds pose before a backdrop of red brick and cobblestone, young families walk their dogs and the fashionable shop for art beneath charmingly decrepit gables and gantries. In summer, expect live jazz, activities, exhibitions and foodie events. (☎416-364-1177; www.thedistillerydistrict.com; 9 Trinity St; ⏰10am-7pm Mon-Wed, to 8pm Thu-Sat, 11am-6pm Sun; 🚌72, 🚋503, 504)

Flatiron Building — HISTORIC BUILDING

2 ◎ MAP P64, B3

An iconic sight in the heart of the old town, the Flatiron is impossible to miss. Built in 1892, it's a five-story iron-shaped building with a steep copper roof and turret; in the background, Toronto's skyscrapers provide a beautiful contrast. Be sure to check out the mural on the building's western side; created by Canadian artist Derek Michael Besant, it integrates with the existing structure to make it appear that a curtain of windows has not been properly tacked up.

Distillery District

A long time office building, the Flatiron was originally built for the Gooderham and Worts Distillery's administrative offices (notably, its repurposed factory serves as the central building of the Distillery District; p65). (Gooderham Building; 49 Wellington St E; 503)

Toronto's First Post Office
HISTORIC SITE

3 MAP P64, A2

Dating from 1834, this national historic site is also the city's oldest surviving post office. A small museum showcases the beginning of the city's postal service back when it was part of the British Royal Mail; the highlight for many is writing a letter with a quill – tougher than it looks! – and posting it. (416-865-1833; https://townofyork.com; 31 Adelaide St E; free; 9am-5:30pm Mon-Fri, 10am-4pm Sat, noon-4pm Sun; Queen)

Eating

Patrician Grill
DINER $

4 MAP P64, C3

Built in the 1950s, the Patrician has been run by the same family since 1967. Photographers will have a field day with the neon outside and the original decor inside. Food centers on burgers, BLTs, bacon and eggs (cooked to perfection) and home fries. Friday-lunchtime meat loaf is a local institution and sells out quickly. (416-366-4841; http://patriciangrill.com; 219 King St E; meals $5-16; 7am-4pm Mon-Fri, 8am-2pm Sat; King)

Schnitzel Queen
EUROPEAN $

5 MAP P64, C1

This poky German takeout specializes in golden-delicious breaded-schnitzel sandwiches that make great picnic fodder. These mammoth creations are excellent value and usually good for two meals – the schnitzel is double the size of the bun. Purists should nab a bar stool and stay in for the authentic dinner plates with mushroom sauce, potato salad and sauerkraut ($11 to $16). (416-504-1311; www.schnitzelqueen.ca; 211 Queen St E; schnitzels $8-12; 11am-9pm Wed, to 10pm Thu & Fri, noon-8pm Sat; 301, 501, 502)

Global Eats in Old York

There's an almost comical variety of cuisines in this compact area of the city: Japanese, German, Indian, Moroccan, a joint that sells a hundred raw oysters for a hundred bucks, a famous-for-its-Friday-meatloaf place, even a restaurant run for and by culinary students. The list goes on, and the majority are reasonably priced and conveniently located.

WORKS Gourmet Burger Bistro
BURGERS $$

6 MAP P64, B3

Everything and anything you could ever want in a burger. All burgers at the Works are completely customizable, including the patty, bun, toppings and sides. There are also more than 50 drool-worthy set options if you'd rather have the choice made for you. (✆416-594-9675; https://worksburger.com; 60 Wellington St E; mains $13-19; ⏲11am-10pm Sun-Wed, to 11pm Thu-Sat; **S** King)

Chef's House
CANADIAN $$

7 MAP P64, C3

Enjoy gourmet fare created and served by culinary students at George Brown College. The dining room is upscale and modern, with an open kitchen (see the team hard at work!). The prix-fixe menu changes regularly, but expect delights like citrus-cured salmon, handmade fettuccine with saffron cream and cardamom crème brûlée. An excellent way to eat well on a tight budget. (✆416-415-2260; www.thechefshouse.com; 215 King St E; 2/3/4 courses from $20/25/41; ⏲11:30am-1pm & 6:30-8:30pm Mon-Fri; **S** King)

Pearl Diver
SEAFOOD $$

8 MAP P64, B2

A small, bustling restaurant, this place is known for its regular seafood specials. Come on Thursday for its crowning glory, the '100 for 100': $100 for 100 raw oysters, quickly and expertly shucked

Feather pen, Toronto's First Post Office

Local Experiences

Art The best time to talk to local artists and check out their **Distillery District studios** (p65) is in the early afternoon – many will have their doors open or signs inviting visitors in.

Eating Join a cooking class or workshop at the **Market Kitchen** (p61), popular with foodies.

Drinking The office crowd packs the house at **Triple A Bar** (p69) most weeknights during happy hour.

(no bits of sand here). On weekends, the lobster benny is where it's at. (416-366-7827; https://pearldiver.to; 100 Adelaide St E; mains $16-44; 4pm-midnight Tue & Wed, 11am-1am Thu-Sat, to midnight Sun; 141, 143, 144, 145)

Nami JAPANESE $$

9 MAP P64, A2

Nami, meaning 'wave' (as in tsunami), is unmissable for its cool blue-neon wave on the outside of the building. Bustling about the black-laquered interior are kimono-clad hostesses and intense sushi chefs, who make only small concessions to North American palates. *Robatayaki* grilling is a specialty, so this is *the* place to try home-style *sukiyaki* hot pot. (416-362-7373; www.namirestaurant.ca; 55 Adelaide St E; lunch sets $18-24, dinner mains from $28, sukiyaki per person $48; 11:45am-2pm & 5:30-10pm Mon-Fri, 5:30-10pm Sat; King)

Drinking

Mill Street Brewery BREWERY

10 MAP P64, F4

With 13 specialty beers made onsite in the atmospheric Distillery District (p65), these guys are a leading light in local microbrewing. Order a sample platter so you can taste all the award-winning brews, including the Tankhouse Pale Ale, Stock Ale and Organic Lager. On a sunny afternoon the courtyard is the place to be. The beer-friendly food includes burgers and wraps. (416-681-0338; www.millstreetbrewery.com; 21 Tank House Lane; 11am-1am Sun-Wed, to 2am Thu-Sat; 72, 503, 504)

C'est What PUB

11 MAP P64, B3

More than 30 whiskeys and six dozen Canadian microbrews (mostly from Ontario) are on hand at this underground pub (look for a doorway). An in-house brewmaster tightly edits the all-natural, preservative-free beers on tap. Good bar food makes the most of fresh produce from St Lawrence Market (p60) next door. (416-867-9499; www.cestwhat.com; 67 Front St E; 11:30am-1am Sun & Mon, to 2am Tue-Sat; 503, 504)

Triple A Bar

BAR

12 MAP P64, B2

Join the after-work crowd for cold-beer-and-shot combos at this busy dive bar. Snag a pleather booth if you can and prepare to lose your voice (the later it is, the louder it gets). If hunger strikes, try the Texas barbecue. (416-850-2726; www.tripleabar.ca; 138 Adelaide St E; noon-2am; 141, 143, 144, 145)

Entertainment

Reservoir Lounge

JAZZ

13 MAP P64, A3

Swing dancers, jazz singers and blues crooners call this cool, candlelit basement lounge home, and it's hosted its fair share of musical greats over the years. Where else can you enjoy a martini while dipping strawberries into chocolate fondue during the show? Tables are reserved for diners; prepare to drop at least $15 per person to sit down. (416-955-0887; www.reservoirlounge.com; 52 Wellington St E; cover $5-10; 7:30pm-2am Tue-Sat; 503, 504)

Soulpepper

THEATER

14 MAP P64, F4

This theater company has a repertoire ranging from new works to classics, most focused on the diversity of Canada's voices and identities. Youth-outreach initiatives and theater training programs are shining stars. Housed in the Young Centre for the Performing Arts (p63) in the heart of

Market Kitchen (p61)

Toronto Light Festival

What better way to get over the winter blues than with a light festival featuring exhibits and performances by local and international artists? The **Toronto Light Festival** (https://torontolightfest.com; 9 Trinity St; free; mid-Jan–early Mar; 72, 503, 504) transforms the Distillery District into a bright urban oasis every year, making winter fun (even if it feels like -20°C outside).

the Distillery District. (416-866-8666; www.soulpepper.ca; 50 Tank House Lane; 503, 504)

CanStage
THEATER

15 MAP P64, D3

Contemporary CanStage produces top-rated Canadian and international plays by the likes of David Mamet and Tony Kushner from its own Berkeley Street Theatre. It's also behind the wonderfully accessible (pay-what-you-can) midsummer productions of Shakespeare in High Park (p119); bring a blanket, show up early and enjoy theater under the stars. (Canadian Stage Company; 416-368-3110; www.canstage.com; 26 Berkeley St; box office 10am-6pm Mon-Sat, show days to 8pm; 503, 504)

Young People's Theatre
THEATER

16 MAP P64, C3

Catch a show at this innovative theater delivering enlightening children's plays and drama camps for more than 50 years. Despite the common misconception, the vast majority of performances are by professional *adult* actors, not child actors. (Lorraine Kimsa Theatre for Young People; 416-862-2222; www.youngpeoplestheatre.ca; 165 Front St E; box office 9am-5pm; 503, 504)

Shopping

Hoi Bo
DESIGN

17 MAP P64, F4

Refined clothing and accessories, all handmade by an in-house crew and using natural materials such as organic wool, bamboo and

Toronto Christmas Market

The Distillery District is at its festive best from mid-November to Christmas Eve during its European-style **Christmas Market** (www.torontochristmasmarket.com; 9 Trinity St; Fri-Sun $6, Tue-Thu free; Tue-Sun mid-Nov–late Dec; 72, 503, 504), showcasing hundreds of local handcrafted products, a carousel and photo ops with Santa.

Christmas Market, Distillery District (p65)

Ontario beeswax. Items aren't cheap, but they're unique and high quality. Think of them as investment pieces. Located in the Distillery District (p65). (📞647-852-5488; www.hoibo.com; 15 Trinity St; ⏰11am-7pm Tue-Sat, to 6pm Sun & Mon; 🚌72, 🚋503, 504)

Gallery Indigena
ART

18 🔒 MAP P64, F4

Specializing in indigenous Canadian art, this Distillery District shop sells original works by Inuit and other indigenous artists, along with some mass-produced artsy gifts. Prices range from museum quality to memento level, which is a plus for those on a tighter budget. Staff members are knowledgeable and ready to share background information about each piece. (📞416-366-3000; www.galleryindigena.com; 46 Gristmill Lane; ⏰noon-6pm daily; 🚌72, 🚋503, 504)

Corktown Designs
JEWELRY

19 🔒 MAP P64, F4

Jewelry is the focus at this Distillery District shop, with case upon glass case of it. Find unique work by locally based artisans and some international folks. Handbags and accessories sold, too. (📞416-861-3020; www.corktowndesigns.com; 5 Trinity St; ⏰10am-7pm Mon-Wed, to 8pm Thu, to 9pm Fri & Sat, 11am-6pm Sun; 🚌72, 🚋503, 504)

Top Sight

Tommy Thompson Park

Once a thin spit of land, Tommy Thompson Park was created when more than 6,500,000 cu meters of sand and silt from the development of Toronto's outer harbor was relocated here. It's a haven for birds – over 316 species have been spotted – and the park is a great place for an outdoorsy walk. Bring binoculars if you can!

416-661-6600

www.tommythompson
park.ca

Leslie St

4-9pm Mon-Fri,
5:30am-9pm Sat & Sun

83 Jones S, 501

Nature Trails

Though Tommy Thompson Park has 18km of trails, only 3.3km are nature trails. Narrow and ungraded, they cross through meadows and along wetlands, affording many more opportunities to see birds and other wildlife than the paved or graded-gravel trails. From the parking lot, follow the multi-use trail until you reach the marina, where the park's first, and longest, nature trail splits off.

Guided Walks

On weekends enthusiastic staff members lead two guided tours through Tommy Thompson Park. The Wildlife Walk typically crosses forests, meadows and wetlands and includes an overview of the park's history and its flora and fauna; the Bird Walk focuses on the park's remarkable birdlife, taking participants to prime bird-watching spots (BYO binoculars). Walks take approximately two hours and leave at 10am from the Nature Centre. Be sure to register online. There's no set fee, but donations are encouraged.

Lighthouse Views

Although the lighthouse itself isn't particularly noteworthy, its position at the tip of Tommy Thompson Park means it has breathtaking views of the Toronto Islands and Toronto's skyline beyond. Located at the end of a pedestrian path, it lies a 10km round-trip from the entrance – a decent walk. Be sure to take provisions!

★ Top Tips

o Birds are visible year-round but are most abundant in May and September, when migration is heaviest.

o The park's paths have relatively little shade, and there's nowhere to buy water or other supplies. Bring a brimmed hat and plenty of water.

o Many locals refer to the park by its old name: the Leslie St Spit, or just 'the Spit.'

✘ Take a Break

Stop at **Gale's Snack Bar** (539 Eastern Ave; meals $2-4; 10am-6pm Mon-Fri, to 5pm Sat; 501, 502, 503) for a quick bite or sandwiches for a picnic in the park.

Alternatively, save your taste buds for a post-visit pint and elevated pub grub at **Rorschach Brewing Co** (416-901-3233; www.rorschachbrewing.com; 1001 Eastern Ave; 5-11pm Mon-Wed, noon-11pm Thu, to midnight Fri & Sat, to 9pm Sun; 301, 501) near the park entrance.

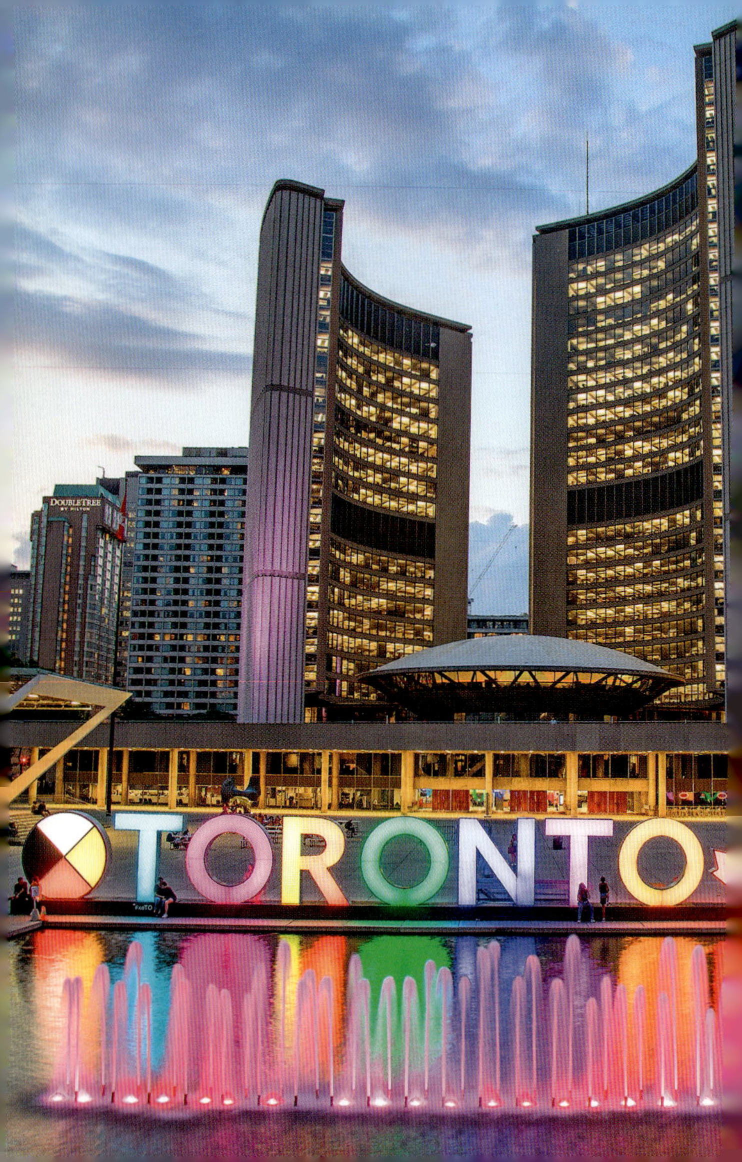
DOUBLETREE BY HILTON
TORONTO

Explore ◈
Downtown Yonge

Toronto's version of Times Sq and San Francisco's Castro district, Downtown Yonge consists of a dense urban strip. At its northern end is Toronto's main gay neighborhood – the Village – unmistakable with its rainbow crosswalks and Pride flags, and home to beloved institutions like Glad Day bookstore and Buddies in Bad Times Theatre. Toronto's distinctive City Hall, the historic Elgin & Winter Garden Theatre and the Eaton Centre mall are also here. At the southern end, the huge Yonge & Dundas Sq lights up the streets with its jumbotrons and occasionally hosts festivals.

The Short List

- **Elgin & Winter Garden Theatre (p76)** Touring Toronto's century-old double-decker theater, the last of its kind.
- **City Hall (p82)** Snapping a pic in front of the iconic 'Toronto' sign with the flying saucer-like city hall in the background.
- **Dirty Bingo at O'Grady's (p86)** Vying for bingo glory at this friendly pub where drag queens call out the numbers.
- **Glad Day (p88)** Browsing the shelves at this iconic bookstore and staying on for the Saturday Night Dance Party.

Getting There & Around

[S] The Yellow line has several stops along Yonge St in downtown, including Queen, Dundas, College and Wellesley stations.

Neighborhood Map on p80

Nathan Phillips Square forms the forecourt to City Hall (p82), by architect Viljo Revell. MIKECPHOTO/SHUTTERSTOCK ©

Top Sight
Elgin & Winter Garden Theatre

The world's last double-decker theater – one theater sits seven stories above the other – that's still in operation, the Elgin & Winter Garden is a sumptuously restored 1913 vaudeville theater with hand-painted walls, botanical-themed ceilings, rich fabrics and gold-leaf decor. Seeing a show here, or even just touring the theater, is a classic Toronto experience.

◎ MAP P80, D8

☏ 416-314-2871

www.heritagetrust.on.ca/ewg

189 Yonge St

tours adult/student $12/10

Ⓢ Queen

Double-Decker Engineering

Designed by New York architect Thomas Lamb in 1913, this double-decker building is an engineering feat: the domed ceiling of the lower Elgin Theatre is suspended by steel rods from the floor of the upper Winter Garden Theatre, high above. As you crane your neck to admire the Elgin's gilded dome, imagine all that lies on the other side!

Winter Garden Floral Ceiling

The Winter Garden Theatre's ceiling is a unique and magical part of the venue's country-garden theme. Based on the original decor, it's made up of more than 5000 beech branches and leaves that were harvested, preserved and painted before being woven into a wire grid high above the seats.

Winter Garden Murals

Two thousand sq meters of original watercolor murals of garden roses, morning glories, ivy and trellises cover the walls of the Winter Garden Theatre – they're impossible to miss. During the theater's restoration in the late 1980s, workers used hundreds of kilograms of bread dough to clean the delicate works of art.

Vaudeville Sets

The Elgin & Winter Garden's array of vaudeville-scenery sets is the largest collection of its kind in the world. Dating from 1913 to 1918, the sets were stowed away in the Winter Garden when it closed in 1928. Custom-made and hand painted at Loew's Scenic Studios in NYC, the sets were discovered during the theater's renovation in the 1980s – a once-in-a-lifetime find. Each theater had its own collection with interchangeable cloth flats, many integrating the art deco and art nouveau styles popular during the vaudeville era. Several are on display in the Theatre Centre.

★ Top Tips

- Avoid the $10-per-ticket service charge by purchasing tickets directly at the box office.

- Rush tickets are available for select shows starting at 9am on performance days; there's a maximum of two tickets per order.

- Tours are cash only; no need to reserve in advance.

✕ Take a Break

Senator Restaurant (p84) has stylish art deco decor and serves home-style classics such as meat loaf, and fish-and-chips.

For something quick, the Eaton Centre's Urban Eatery (p84) is across the street from the theaters, and has more than 45 eateries.

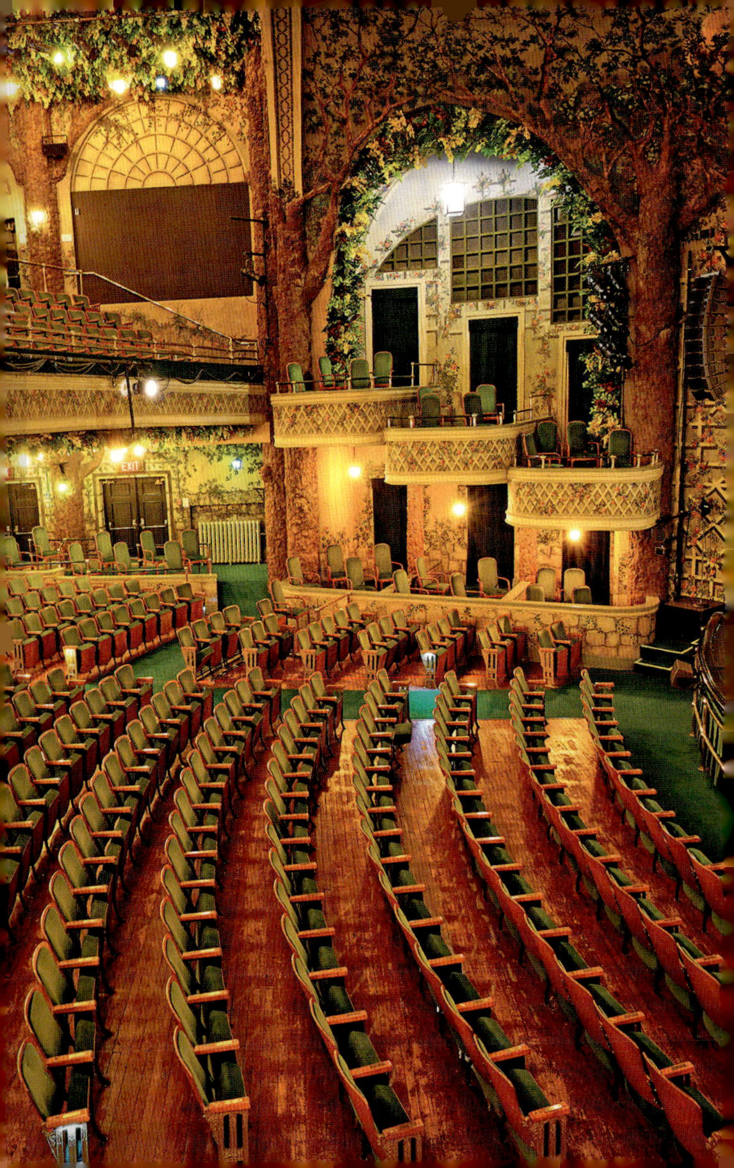
EXIT

Theatre History

The Elgin & Winter Garden Theatres, elegant and plush, were built to serve as the Canadian flagship of the Loew's chain of vaudeville theaters. Each was designed with a different audience in mind: the Winter Garden Theatre, the upper and more exclusive one, had big-ticket shows and reserved seating. The Elgin Theatre (then called Loew's Yonge Street Theatre) was much larger, with more than 1500 seats, and was used for less-renowned acts and silent films. Despite the theaters' initial popularity, the advent of talkies (pictures with sound) led to the closure of the Winter Garden just 15 years after it opened. It remained shuttered for over 50 years. Meanwhile, the Elgin was converted into a movie house, and by the 1970s it was used mostly to screen low-budget films.

Enter the Ontario Heritage Trust. Tasked with protecting and preserving Canada's cultural heritage, the government agency purchased the property in 1981. A year later the theaters were designated a national historic site. The trust spearheaded efforts to restore them, raising $29 million in private and public funds. Though the Elgin quickly re-emerged as a legitimate venue (a successful production of Broadway musical *Cats* ran from 1985 to 1987), the trust closed the theaters for complete restoration and renovation. The project lasted three years – but it was worth the wait. Today the theaters serve as reminders of the city's past through sumptuous color and delightful detail.

Left: Winter Garden Theatre

Downtown Yonge

YORKVILLE

YONGE ST STRIP

CHURCH-WELLESLEY VILLAGE

Downtown Yonge

For reviews see
- 🔴 Top Sights — p76
- 🟢 Sights — p82
- ❌ Eating — p82
- 🔵 Drinking — p86
- 🟠 Entertainment — p88
- 🟣 Shopping — p88

Top Sights
- City Hall (1)
- Textile Museum of Canada (2)
- Church of the Holy Trinity (3)
- Elgin & Winter Garden Theatre

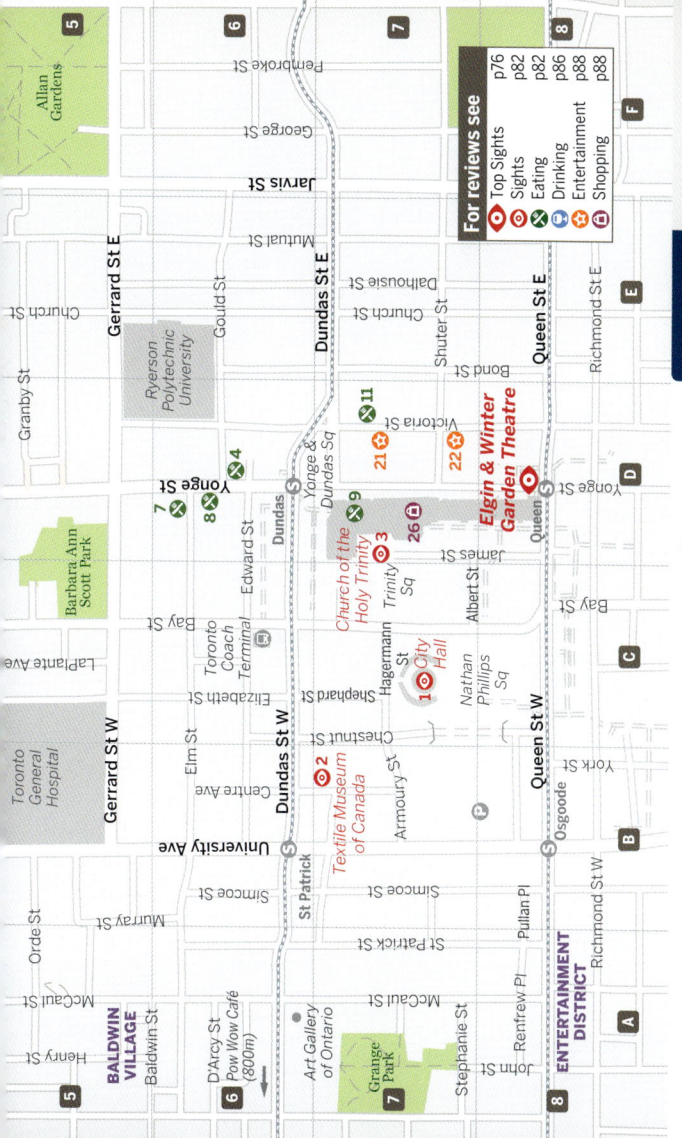

Neighborhoods
- BALDWIN VILLAGE
- ENTERTAINMENT DISTRICT

Parks & Landmarks
- Allan Gardens
- Ryerson Polytechnic University
- Barbara Ann Scott Park
- Toronto General Hospital
- Toronto Coach Terminal
- Nathan Phillips Sq
- Yonge & Dundas Sq
- Art Gallery of Ontario
- Grange Park
- Pow Wow Café (800m)

Numbered locations
- 4, 7, 8, 9, 11 (Eating)
- 21, 22 (Entertainment)
- 26 (Shopping)

Streets
Church St, Granby St, Bay St, Yonge St, Victoria St, Bond St, Church St, Shuter St, Dalhousie St, Mutual St, Jarvis St, George St, Pembroke St, Gerrard St E, Gould St, Dundas St E, Queen St E, Richmond St E, LaPlante Ave, Elizabeth St, Edward St, Bay St, James St, Albert St, Hagerman St, Shepherd St, Chestnut St, Centre Ave, Armoury St, York St, Dundas St W, Queen St W, University Ave, St Patrick St, Simcoe St, Pulan Pl, Richmond St W, Orde St, Murray St, McCaul St, Henry St, Baldwin St, D'Arcy St, Stephanie St, John St, Renfrew Pl, Elm St, Gerrard St W

Sights

City Hall
HISTORIC BUILDING

1 ◎ MAP P80, C7

Much-maligned City Hall was Toronto's bold leap into architectural modernity. Its twin clamshell towers, central 'flying saucer,' ramps and mosaics were completed in 1965 to Finnish architect Viljo Revell's award-winning design. An irritable Frank Lloyd Wright compared it to a gravestone; Revell died before construction was finished. At the info desk you can collect a self-guided tour pamphlet with points of interest, including a stunning artwork by Norval Morrisseau, one of Canada's most revered indigenous painters. (☏311, 416-392-2489; www.toronto.ca; 100 Queen St W; free; ⊙8:30am-4:30pm Mon-Fri; P; SQueen)

Textile Museum of Canada
MUSEUM

2 ◎ MAP P80, B7

Tucked into a condo tower, this small museum has exhibits drawing on its permanent collection of more than 13,000 items from Latin America, Africa, Europe, Southeast Asia and India, as well as contemporary Canada. Workshops teach batik making, weaving, knitting and needlecraft; many are included in the price of admission. (☏416-599-5321; www.textilemuseum.ca; 55 Centre Ave; adult/child $15/free, 5-8pm Wed by donation; ⊙11am-5pm Thu-Tue, to 8pm Wed, tours 2pm Sun; SSt Patrick)

Church of the Holy Trinity
CHURCH

3 ◎ MAP P80, D7

Tucked away behind the west side of the gargantuan Eaton Centre (p89) is the oasis-like Trinity Sq, named after the welcoming Anglican Church of the Holy Trinity. When it opened in 1847 it was the first church in Toronto not to charge parishioners for pews. Today, it's notable for welcoming same-sex marriage ceremonies and is a cross between a house of worship, a small concert venue and a community drop-in center – everything a downtown church should be! (☏416-598-4521; www.holytrinitytoronto.org; 10 Trinity Sq; ⊙11am-3pm Mon-Fri, 8am-2pm Sun, services 12:15pm Wed, 10:30am & 2pm Sun; SDundas)

Eating

Outdoor Eateries
FOOD TRUCK $

4 ◎ MAP P80, D6

Food trucks, repurposed shipping containers and plywood sheds make up this outdoor food court at the heart of Yonge St. Short-order cooks prep burritos, Philly cheesesteak subs, crepes, vegan eats and more. Hungry diners (many of them students from nearby Ryerson University) fill the picnic tables in the center courtyard. Twinkling lights set the mood in the evening. (335 Yonge St; mains from $3; ⊙11am-10:30pm; ✎; SDundas, College)

Local Experiences

Drag queens
- Dirty Bingo at **O'Grady's** (p86) and Sunday Drag Brunch at **Glad Day** (p88) are the most popular of the many drag-related events in the Village. (Arrive early!)

Outdoor eats
- In the warmer months, join office workers and students for lunch at Fresh Wednesdays in front of **City Hall** or the **Outdoor Eateries** (p82) near Ryerson University.

Shopping
- Instead of hitting the international chains in the **Eaton Centre** (p89), do as locals do and hit the neighborhood shops, like **Dead Dog Records** (p89).

Loblaw's SUPERMARKET $
5 MAP P80, E4

Yeah, it's a grocery-store chain, but this flagship is a must-stop for its high-quality prepared-foods section: sushi made to order, grilled meats, thin-crust pizza, creative sandwiches and salads...and don't miss the killer patisserie and Wall of Cheese. Plenty of seating and occasional live music. Ninety minutes of free parking, too. (416-593-6154; 60 Carlton St; mains from $3; 7am-11pm; P; S College)

Okonomi House JAPANESE $
6 MAP P80, C1

Okonomi House is one of the only places in Toronto, and perhaps North America, dishing up authentic *okonomiyaki* (savory Japanese cabbage pancakes filled with meat, seafood or vegetables). It's not fancy – just a step up from a diner – but it's a must for Japanophiles. (416-925-6176; 23 Charles St W; mains $9-17; 11:30am-3pm & 4:30-10pm Mon-Fri, noon-3pm & 4:30-10pm Sat; S Bloor-Yonge)

Patties Express JAMAICAN $
7 MAP P80, D6

A hole-in-the-wall place specializing in Jamaican patties: flaky-pastry pockets stuffed with spicy veggies, curry chicken and ground beef (non-spicy to extra spicy available). For a one-two punch to your taste buds, order your patty spicy and wrapped in coconut bread. Takeout only. (647-350-0111; www.pattiesexpress.ca; 4 Elm St; patties from $2; 10:30am-11pm Mon-Fri, 11am-11pm Sat, to 9pm Sun; S Dundas, College)

Doors Open Toronto

Over the fourth weekend of May, several public and private buildings of architectural and historical significance creak open their doors, allowing you to sneak a free peek at what's hot and what's not in other people's digs. Book ahead for walking tours and big-name buildings such as **City Hall** (p82) and **Union Station** (p47).

Salad King   THAI $
8 MAP P80, D6

An institution among students of neighboring Ryerson University, the colorful and somewhat misleadingly named Salad King dispenses large bowls of standard Thai curries, noodle soups, rice and, yes, salads, for around $12. Long stainless-steel shared tables and cozy booths are usually full of hungry patrons. You can specify your desired level of spice on a scale of one to 20! (416-593-0333; www.saladking.com; 340 Yonge St; mains $11-13; 11am-10pm Mon-Thu, to 11pm Fri, noon-11pm Sat, to 9pm Sun; S Dundas)

Urban Eatery   FOOD HALL $
9 MAP P80, D7

More than just a food court, the Urban Eatery, in the basement of the gargantuan Eaton Centre (p89), has more than 45 outlets, from fast food to seated dining. If you're in a pinch for something to eat and you're tired of walking, you're bound to find something here; in fact, you'll be spoiled for choice. (1 Dundas St W; mains from $5; 10am-9pm Mon-Sat, to 7pm Sun; S Dundas)

Smith   CANADIAN $$
10 MAP P80, E2

Come to this bohemian-chic eatery in the heart of the Village for brunch, when the classics are served with flair: eggs Benedict with leek fondue, a short stack with maple cream cheese and candied lemon, or perhaps a Bloody Mary with a bouquet of bacon on top. Is your mouth watering yet? Reservations recommended. (416-926-2501; http://smithrestaurant.com; 553 Church St; mains $18-28; 11am-4pm & 5-11pm Tue-Thu, to midnight Fri, 9am-4pm & 5pm-midnight Sat, 9am-4pm Sun; S Wellesley)

Senator Restaurant   DINER $$
11 MAP P80, D7

Art deco buffs will delight in the Senator's curved glass windows, fluted aluminum counter face and original booths. Meals are refreshingly simple and home style: the fish-and-chips, meat loaf and macaroni are especially recommended. On weekends, head upstairs to its wine bar, **Top O' the Senator**, for drinks and live jazz until midnight. (416-364-7517; www.thesenator.com; 249 Victoria St;

mains $18-36; 7:30am-2:30pm Mon. to 9pm Tue-Fri, 8am-2:30pm & 4:30-9pm Sat, 8am-2:30pm Sun; S Dundas)

Hair of the Dog PUB FOOD $$

12 MAP P80, E4

At its best in the warmer months, when two levels of shaded patio spring to life with a gay and straight crowd, this chilled puppy is delightfully less mainstream than its Village neighbors a few blocks north. Equally tempting as a drinking venue, the Dog serves great sharing plates and salads, too. No nonvegetarian can possibly resist the butter-chicken grilled cheese. (416-964-2708; www.hairofdogpub.com; 425 Church St; share plates $12-20, mains $15-24; 11:30am-midnight Mon-Thu, to 2am Fri, 10:30am-2am Sat, to midnight Sun; S College)

Wish Restaurant CANADIAN $$

13 MAP P80, D2

There's no need to get out of the city to experience beach vibes. Wish is a South Beach–inspired restaurant serving up delicious Canadian comfort food and brunch, including lots of vegetarian and vegan options. The gorgeous patio is heated during the colder months, so you can enjoy it year-round. (416-935-0240; http://wishintoronto.com; 3 Charles St E; mains $19-22; 11:30am-11pm Tue-Fri, 10am-3pm & 5-11pm Sat, 10am-4pm Sun; ; S Bloor-Yonge)

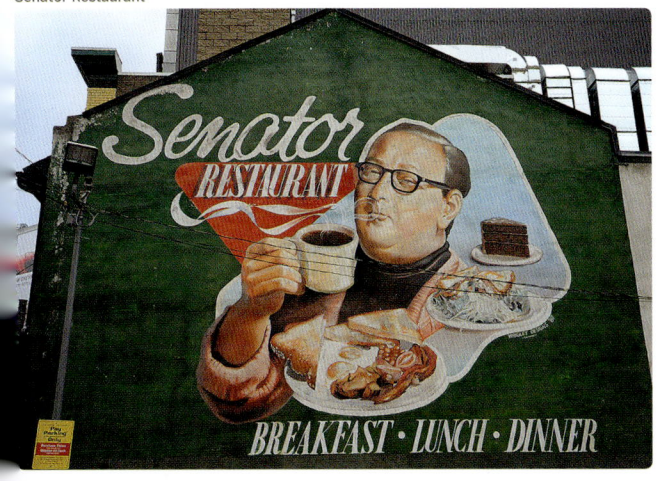

Senator Restaurant

First Nations Heritage & History

Toronto is built on the ancestral lands of several First Nations communities: the Mississauga of the New Credit, the Anishnabeg, the Chippewa, the Wendat and the Haudenosaunee. The latter's name translates roughly as 'people who live in the extended longhouses'; indeed, indigenous communities in this region were known for their distinctive curved-roof houses, covered in bark and animal skins, and up to 100m long – space enough for the 20 family 'apartments' within.

Indigenous warriors were recruited into various conflicts between French, British and American colonists, often to decisive effect. But their communities were repaid in misery, including broken treaties, starvation and disease; today more than 90% of First Nations Torontonians live at or below poverty level. First Nations activists have won important victories in their long fight to expose and rectify ancient (and not-so-ancient) wrongs; prime ministers have apologized for cultural genocide, a Truth and Reconciliation Commission laid out a series of recommendations, and legal damages have been paid to survivors of forced adoptions, residential schools and other atrocities.

The exact population of First Nations people in Toronto is difficult to determine; the latest census says 45,000, but service agencies say it's closer to 70,000. Of course, the cultures of First Nations peoples are more than their wrenching history; they're also art, food, celebrations and more, with many First Nations' locales dotting the city. Check out **Pow Wow Café** (p97) for traditional food, the **Art Gallery of Ontario** (p92) for works of art, and **Native Canadian Centre of Toronto** (p109) for weekly cultural events and seasonal powwows.

Drinking

O'Grady's   PUB

14   MAP P80, E3

Come to this friendly Irish pub on Wednesdays for Dirty Bingo nights, when fabulous drag queens call out numbers and give winners risqué prizes from 9pm to midnight. On bingo-less nights, it's all about the patio – the Village's largest – which fills up as soon as the sun comes out. The kitchen, serving comfort food, stays open late. (416-323-2822; www.ogradyschurch.com; 517 Church St; 11am-2am; Wellesley)

One Eighty
BAR

15 MAP P80, C1

Swanky and priced to match, the city's highest licensed patio has arguably Toronto's best views outside the CN Tower. It's in the Manulife Centre, a mall and residential building, and unlike the tower, it has no admission fee, though you're well advised to drop some cash on a martini or a meal. Look for the elevators next to the Cineplex. (416-967-0000; www.the51stfloor.com; Manulife Centre, 55 Bloor St W, 51st fl; 5pm-midnight Mon-Thu, to 2am Fri & Sat, 11am-midnight Fri-Sun; S Bay)

Storm Crow Manor
BAR

16 MAP P80, E2

Geek out at this Victorian mansion turned bar with sci-fi themed rooms, board games and dungeon masters. Drinks come in all shapes and sizes, including beakers and Darth Vadar heads (dry ice and light-up ice cubes figure strongly). Hearty pub grub is served; roll the dice, literally, to pick your meal and sides. (416-367-2769; www.stormcrow.com; 580 Church St; 11am-11pm Sun-Wed, to midnight Thu, to 2am Fri & Sat; S Wellesley)

Crews & Tangos
BAR

17 MAP P80, E4

A sprawling bar that becomes a crowded nightclub on weekends, Crews & Tangos features live drag and cabaret shows and DJs out back. Boys who like boys, girls who like girls, girlish boys and boyish girls and all their friends tend to make up the lively crowd in this welcoming space. Look for the blue brick house with the murals. (647-349-7469; www.crewsandtangos.com; 508 Church St; 8pm-2am Sun-Fri, 6pm-2am Sat; S Wellesley)

Black Eagle
GAY

18 MAP P80, E4

Men-only Eagle lures leather-men, uniform fetishists and their admirers. The year-round rooftop patio is the perfect place to meet a Daddy; Sunday-afternoon barbecues draw a strong crowd. There's a cruising area upstairs and a renovated dance area downstairs. While it's not for the fainthearted, the folks here are generally as friendly as they come. (416-413-1219; www.blackeagletoronto.com; 457 Church St; 3pm-3am Mon-Sat, to midnight Sun; S Wellesley)

> ### LGBTIQ+ Pride Fest
>
> **Pride Toronto** (www.pridetoronto.com; Jun) is one of the city's most well-attended festivals, celebrating diversity of sexuality and gender identity with a whole month of community events, workshops and gatherings – all mostly free. The celebration ends big with a Trans March, Dyke March and Pride Parade, when the streets around the Village heave with over a million revelers.

Woody's/Sailor — BAR

19 MAP P80, E4

Toronto's most well-known gay bar is a sprawling complex with a grab bag of tricks, from drag shows, 'best ass' contests and billiard tables to nightly DJs. Sailor is a slick bar off to one side. Popular with the 30- and 40-something crowd. (416-972-0887; www.woodystoronto.com; 465-467 Church St; 1pm-2am; SWellesley)

Entertainment

Buddies in Bad Times Theatre — THEATER

20 MAP P80, D4

Founded in 1979, Buddies is the world's oldest queer theater company. Its mission: to develop and produce queer voices and stories on stage. Check the website for programming; pay-what-you-can tickets are available for some shows. Late night on weekends the theater opens its bar, **Tallulah's**, where proceeds from dance parties, drag shows and other events are used to support the theater. (416-975-8555; http://buddiesinbadtimes.com; 12 Alexander St; SWellesley)

Ed Mirvish Theatre — THEATER

21 MAP P80, D7

Formerly the Canon, the Ed Mirvish Theatre was renamed in 2011 in honor of the late Ed Mirvish, a well-loved Toronto businessman, philanthropist and patron of the arts. One of four Mirvish theaters, the 1920s-era vaudeville hall is a hot ticket for musical extravaganzas. Rush tickets are available for same-day performances only and are limited to two per person. (416-872-1212; www.mirvish.com; 244 Victoria St; SDundas)

Massey Hall — CONCERT VENUE

22 MAP P80, D7

Few venues have hosted as diverse a range of performances as Massey Hall, with over 125 years in the business. Extensive renovations to bring the 2500-seat space into the next generation while retaining its period charm began in July 2018; the projected end date is 2020. (416-872-4255; www.masseyhall.com; 178 Victoria St; box office from noon show days only; SQueen)

Shopping

Glad Day — BOOKS

23 MAP P80, E3

It's the oldest still-running gay bookstore in the world, making Glad Day an LGBTIQ landmark. The store has transformed from a place to defy censorship of LGBTIQ publications into an event and gathering space to promote creativity and further free speech. It's also a cafe and bar. Weekends mean Saturday-night dance parties and Sunday Drag Brunch. (416-901-6600; www.gladdaybookshop.com; 499 Church St; 10am-10pm Mon-Thu, to 2am Fri & Sat, 11am-7pm Sun; SWellesley)

Dead Dog Records MUSIC
24 MAP P80, E3

A small used-record store with a good, well-organized selection of vinyls, CDs and even cassette tapes. Check out the merch from long-past concerts and don't leave without digging through the $2 bins – there are finds to be had! (647-325-4575; www.deaddogrecords.ca; 568 Church St; noon-8pm Tue-Thu, 11am-7pm Sat, noon-6pm Sun; S Wellesley)

Out on the Street ADULT
25 MAP P80, E2

Three floors of LGBTIQ-oriented merch, sex toys and Pride Canada souvenirs. A great place to get rainbow briefs, a dildo or a Pride mug…something for everyone!
(416-967-2759; 551 Church St; 10am-8pm Mon-Wed, to 9pm Thu-Sat, 11am-7pm Sun; S Wellesley)

Eaton Centre MALL
26 MAP P80, D7

Located between two subway stations and opposite Yonge & Dundas Sq, downtown Toronto's largest shopping mall has branches of almost every large retailer in North America, and some not-so-well-known local stores. Constantly full of people milling about and thinning their wallets, its enormous light-filled atrium is a haven on cold winter days. (416-598-8560; www.torontoeatoncentre.com; 220 Yonge St; 10am-9:30pm Mon-Fri, 9:30am-9:30pm Sat, 10am-7pm Sun; S Queen, Dundas)

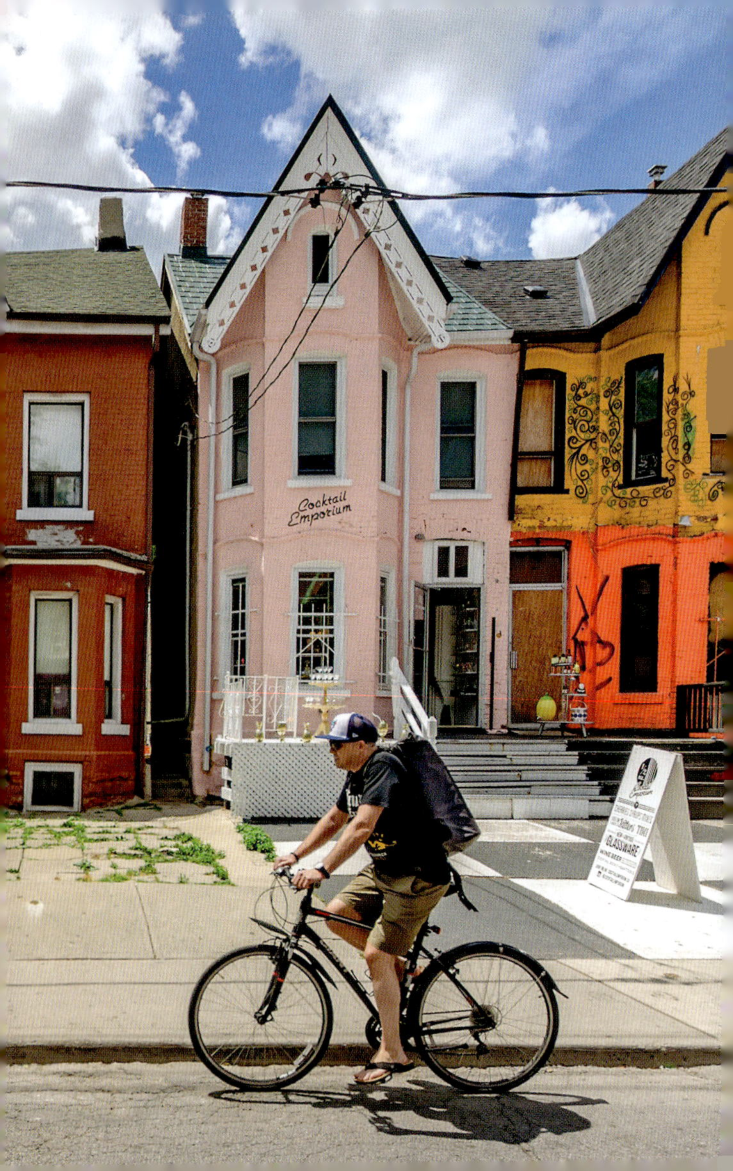
Cocktail Emporium

Explore
Kensington Market & Chinatown

Tattered around the edges, elegantly wasted Kensington Market is Toronto at its most interesting. It's not a constrained market as much as a working residential neighborhood. You'll find flavors from around the world and pocket-size vintage stores, bikers and dreadlocked urbanites, artists and anarchists getting along just fine. Adjacent to Kensington Market, straddling busy Spadina Ave, is Chinatown, with its hectic restaurants, small groceries and curio shops.

The Short List

- **Art Gallery of Ontario (p92)** Ogling an impressive collection of artwork from all over Canada.

- **Foodie heaven (p96)** Noshing on dishes from across the world, from Hong Kong congee to Baja-style fish tacos.

- **Vintage shopping (p100)** Discovering vintage clothing, accessories and more at sought-after thrift shops.

- **Live music (p99)** Listening to live music at neighborhood performance spaces like the legendary Horseshoe Tavern, still drawing crowds after 70 years.

Getting There & Around

[S] The Yellow line has several stops along the eastern edge of the neighborhood.

Streetcar 310 and 510 run north–south on Spadina Ave, 505 runs east–west along Dundas St, and 306 and 506 run east–west along College St.

Neighborhood Map on p94

Cycling through Kensington Market
MARC BRUXELLE/ALAMY STOCK PHOTO ©

Top Sight
Art Gallery of Ontario

A work of art itself, the Art Gallery of Ontario is a spectacular building reminiscent of a crystal ship. It holds a remarkable collection of more than 80,000 works, with a focus on Canadian art from colonial times to the present. There are several floors, corridors and galleries, so consider taking a free tour to help you navigate the place.

◎ MAP P94, G4

AGO

www.ago.net

317 Dundas St W

adult/under 25yr $25/free, 6-9pm Wed free

⏲ 10:30am-5pm Tue & Thu, to 9pm Wed & Fri, to 5:30pm Sat & Sun

🚋 505

Indigenous & Canadian Art Collection

Set on the 1st and 2nd floors, the AGO's Indigenous & Canadian Art collection is a must-see. Spanning centuries, it includes works by some of the country's greats: from landscapes by Tom Thomson and the Group of Seven to huge canvases by First Nations painter Norval Morrisseau. The range of pieces – sculptures, carvings, wall hangings, photographs, works on paper – is astounding.

Henry Moore Sculpture Centre

Opened in 1974, the 2nd-floor Henry Moore Sculpture Centre houses the world's largest public collection of this monumental artist's creations: more than 900 sculptures and works on paper. Most of the pieces were donated to the AGO by Moore himself – a remarkable gift. Allow some time to take in the artist's works and explore the multimedia exhibits that share the inspiration behind the art.

Architecture & Design

As notable as the works of art inside, the AGO building itself is well worth admiring. The original building, dating from 1900, has been renovated and expanded several times. Perhaps the most striking update was the 2008 redesign by renowned Canadian architect Frank Gehry. The almost dreamlike new elements include the stunning entrance, a curving glass wall reminiscent of a crystal ship that reflects the Victorian houses across the way; the Walker Court's spiraling **baroque staircase**, a wooden curlicue rising through a glass ceiling seemingly to the clouds; and the breathtaking **Galleria Italia**, its tall, curving wooden beams and floor-to-ceiling windows calling to mind the hull of a ship or the inside of a whale.

★ Top Tips

- Excellent museum tours, from hour-long overviews to 10-minute 'On the Dot' discussions about a single artwork, are always free with admission.

- AGO has terrific youth programming, including two roving maker stations and engaging DIY art projects in the Dr Mariano Elia Hands-On Centre.

- Admission is free on Wednesday evenings; arrive after 6pm and leave your backpack at the hotel to avoid queues.

- Admission is always free for anyone aged 25 and under.

✕ Take a Break

The museum's upscale **AGO Bistro** specializes in innovative dishes, often designed to pair with a special exhibit.

For a mid-visit cappuccino, stop at the **Espresso Bar** in **Galleria Italia**, a gorgeous, light-filled room reminiscent of the hull of a ship.

Kensington Market & Chinatown

For reviews see
- 🎯 Top Sights — p92
- ✖ Eating — p96
- 🍷 Drinking — p98
- ⭐ Entertainment — p99
- 🛍 Shopping — p100

Kensington Market & Chinatown

University of Toronto (St George Campus) · College St · Queens Park

400 m / 0.2 miles

Ross St · Cecil St · Beverley St · Henry St · Orde St · McCaul St · Murray St · University Ave

BALDWIN VILLAGE

Baldwin St · Elm St · D'Arcy St

Dundas St W — 22

Art Gallery of Ontario · St Patrick

Grange Ave · Grange Pl · Beverley St · Grange Park · McCaul St · St Patrick St · Simcoe St · University Ave

Sullivan St · Phoebe St · Stephanie St

Bulwer St · Soho St · John St · **ENTERTAINMENT DISTRICT** · Renfrew Pl · Pullan Pl

23 · Queen St W · 16 · Osgoode

Eating

House of Gourmet HONG KONG $

1 MAP P94, D4

A popular, fluorescent-bulb-lit restaurant specializing in Hong Kong–style congee, noodles, barbecue and seafood – more than 800 dishes of them! (It takes two menus with tiny font to cover the options.) Food comes out fast and piping hot. Service is equally brisk. If in doubt, try the wonton-brisket-noodle soup, a late-night fave with chunks of tender brisket and loads of noodles. (416-640-0103; http://houseofgourmet.blogspot.com; 484 Dundas St W; mains $8-19; 8am-2am; 310, 510)

Parka Food Co. VEGAN

2 MAP P94, C6

A starkly white, casual restaurant serving insanely delicious vegan comfort food: burgers made from marinated portobello mushrooms and blackened cauliflower; mac 'n' (vegan) cheese with toppings like truffle mushroom and garlic and onion; and thick, flavorful soups. Everything's made in-house, from scratch, using locally sourced ingredients. Lots of gluten-free options, too. (416-603-3363; www.parkafoodco.com; 424 Queen St W; 11:30am-9pm Mon-Thu, to 10pm Fri, noon-10pm Sat, to 8pm Sun;)

Budget eats in Kensington Market

Pow Wow Café NATIVE AMERICAN

3 MAP P94, B3

A cozy, boho eatery with streetfront seating, Pow Wow serves Ojibwe dishes, mostly fry-bread tacos with a choice of fillings such as beef chili, veggie, coconut-curry chicken or pork souvlaki. Start with a bowl of corn soup with smoked duck or order a salad with edible flowers. Cash only. (416-551-7717; 213 Augusta Ave; tacos from $15; 11am-8pm; 310, 510)

Seven Lives TACOS $

4 MAP P94, C3

What started as a pop-up taqueria is now a hole-in-the-wall place with lines of people snaking out the door, waiting to order Baja-style fish tacos: light and flaky mahi-mahi with pico de gallo, cabbage and a creamy sauce. Other seafood and veggie combos offered, too. Most diners eat standing or take their meal to nearby Bellevue Sq. (416-803-1086; 69 Kensington Ave; tacos from $6; noon-6pm Mon-Fri, to 7pm Sat & Sun; 310, 510)

Nguyen Huong SANDWICHES $

5 MAP P94, D3

Cheap and delicious filled Vietnamese sandwiches are the order of the day at the original precursor to Toronto's banh mi (baguettes filled with pâté, cilantro, pork and pickled veg) phenomenon. Takeout only. (416-599-4625; www.nguyenhuong.ca; 322 Spadina Ave; sandwiches from $3; 8:30am-8:30pm; 510)

Mother's Dumplings CHINESE $

6 MAP P94, D1

The cleanest and best located of Chinatown's dumpling houses prepares plump and juicy dumplings to authentic recipes passed on down generations. However you like them – steamed or panfried; pork, chicken, beef, shrimp or vegetarian – these dumplings will fill your tum and delight your wallet. Always busy. (416-217-2008; www.mothersdumplings.com; 421 Spadina Ave; 10 dumplings from $11; 11:30am-10pm Sun-Thu, to 10:30pm Fri & Sat; ; 506, 510)

Swatow CHINESE $

7 MAP P94, D3

Catering to a late-night crowd, the menu here covers cuisine from Swatow (a city now known as Shantou, on the coast of China's Guangdong province). The house noodles are fiery and prepared in a style nicknamed 'red cooking' for its potent splashes of fermented rice wine. Cash only; be prepared to queue. (416-977-0601; 309 Spadina Ave; mains $8-16; 11am-2am; 505, 510)

FIKA Cafe CAFE $

8 MAP P94, C3

Meaning 'coffee break' in Swedish, FIKA is a small cafe in a turquoise Victorian house. Inside, the decor is soothing: exposed-brick walls, whitewashed wood and artful touches such as open books doubling as wallpaper. The menu's limited to fresh salads and creative sandwiches, though its coffee and homemade-pastry offerings are impressive. Try the cinnamon buns. (www.fika.ca; 28 Kensington Ave; mains from $6; ⏰10am-6pm Mon-Sat; 📶✏️; 🚋310, 510)

Dipped Donuts
BAKERY $

9 MAP P94, C2

A *tiny* shop selling freshly made, light, moist and fluffy doughnuts with innovative toppings and glazes. Not into lemon-poppyseed glaze with blueberry-mint drizzle? How about rosewater pistachio nut or chocolate ganache with cookie crumble? Apple fritters, with big chunks of apple, are sold on weekends. Vegan doughnuts sold, too. Come early…the goodies often sell out. Cash only. (📞647-906-3668; www.dippeddonuts.ca; 161 Baldwin St; doughnuts from $3.25; ⏰10am-6pm Sun-Thu, to 7pm Fri & Sat; 🚋310, 510)

Kekou
ICE CREAM $

10 MAP P94, D6

Whiskey, black-sesame or oolong tea: no, they're not cocktails but excellent, Asian-inspired ice creams. The delicious flavors aren't overly sweet or artificial, and the ginger and dark-chocolate dairy free is the punchiest vegan gelato in Toronto. Cold tea drinks – steeped to order and served with tapioca, grass jelly or gelato – are offered, too. (📞416-792-8858; http://kekou.ca; 394 Queen St W; gelato from $5, drinks from $6; ⏰12:30-10:30pm Sun-Thu, to 11pm Fri & Sat; ✏️; 🚋301, 310, 501, 510)

Drinking

BarChef
COCKTAIL BAR

11 MAP P94, B6

You'll hear 'oohs' and 'aahs' coming from the tables in the intimate near-darkness of this swanky bar

---

Local Experiences

Eating late

◦ Late-night dining in Chinatown is definitely a thing; head to **House of Gourmet** (p96) to rub elbows with locals of all stripes.

Grazing

◦ Kensington Market is a parade of hole-in-the-wall eateries, such as **Seven Lives** (p97) and **Dipped Donuts**. Move from place to place trying different flavors and cuisines.

Parking

◦ During the week there are often open spots in the **parking garage** on Baldwin near Kensington. On weekends, don't bother driving. Streetcars stop along Spadina, just a block away.

Street ARToronto

While there's definitely a singular pleasure in 'discovering' street art on unexpected buildings and down random alleys, for a more purposeful exploration check out StART's website (https://streetartoronto.ca). It includes a super-handy database and map, with the locations of hundreds of paintings and murals, searchable by neighborhood.

---

as cocktails emerge alongside a bonsai tree, or under a bell jar of vanilla and hickory-wood smoke. Beyond novelty, drinks show incredible, enticing complexity without overwhelming some unique flavors – truffle snow, chamomile syrup, cedar air, and soil! (☏416-868-4800; www.barcheftoronto.com; 472 Queen St W; cocktails $16-55; ⏱6pm-2am; Ⓢ Osgoode)

Handlebar   BAR

12 🚊 MAP P94, B3

A jolly little spot paying homage to the bicycle and its lovers, from owners with a fine pedigree. In a great spot in south Kensington Market, there's some wonderful retro styling and a nice mix of shiny happy punters. A calendar of quirky hipster events makes it an easier bar to visit if you're traveling solo. (☏647-748-7433; www.thehandlebar.ca; 159 Augusta Ave; ⏱7pm-2am; 🚊505)

Velvet Underground   CLUB

13 🚊 MAP P94, A6

The place for those who prefer not to spend their nights listening to overplayed top-40 songs. Formerly an industrial club, it's the spot to get your alt-rock on, with DJs and live bands. (☏647-351-9001; http://thevelvet.ca; 508 Queen St W; 🚊501)

Moonbean Coffee Company   COFFEE

14 🚊 MAP P94, C3

'Nothing here is just ordinary,' says the dude behind the counter, and that's true. Serving the best latte west of Yonge St, Moonbean has organic and fair-trade coffees, all-day breakfasts for around $6, and 'Bite Me' vegan cookies. Grind-your-own beans from $16 per pound. Looseleaf teas sold, too. (☏416-595-0327; www.moonbeamcoffee.com; 30 St Andrew St; coffees from $3; ⏱7am-8pm; 🚊510)

Entertainment

Horseshoe Tavern   LIVE MUSIC

15 ⭐ MAP P94, D6

Well past its 70th birthday, the legendary Horseshoe still plays a crucial role in the development of local indie rock. This place oozes a history of good times and classic performances. Come for a beer and check it out. (☏416-598-4226; www.horseshoetavern.com; 370 Queen St W; ⏱noon-2:30am; 🚊501, 510)

Weekend Revelry

The last Sunday of the month from May to October, Augusta Ave and the surrounding streets are pedestrian only to make room for the crowds, food vendors, live music and general revelry in Kensington Market.

Rex
JAZZ

16 MAP P94, G6

The Rex has risen from its pugilistic, blue-collar past to become an outstanding jazz and blues venue. Over a dozen Dixieland, experimental and other local and international acts knock over the joint each week. Cheap drinks; affordable cover. (416-598-2475; www.therex.ca; 194 Queen St W; shows 6:30pm & 9:30pm Mon-Thu, 4pm, 6:30pm & 9:45pm Fri, noon, 3:30pm, 7pm & 9:45pm Sat & Sun; 501)

Theatre Passe Muraille
THEATER

17 MAP P94, A6

Since the 1960s the Theatre Passe Muraille, in the old Nasmith's Bakery & Stables, has focused on radical new plays with contemporary Canadian themes. Post-performance chats with the cast and producers occur often. Saturday and Sunday matinees are pay what you can. (Theater Beyond Walls; 416-504-7529; www.passemuraille.on.ca; 16 Ryerson Ave; Oct-Apr; 501)

Cameron House
LIVE MUSIC

18 MAP P94, C6

Singer-songwriters, soul, jazz and country performers grace this boho stage; artists, musos, dreamers and slackers crowd both front and back rooms. Look for the building with the colorful murals. (416-703-0811; www.thecameron.com; 408 Queen St W; 4pm-2am Mon-Sat, 6pm-2am Sun; 501, 510)

Shopping

Courage My Love
VINTAGE

19 MAP P94, C4

Vintage-clothing stores have been around Kensington Market for decades, but Courage My Love amazes fashion mavens with its secondhand slip dresses, retro pants and white dress shirts in a cornucopia of styles. The beads, buttons, leather goods and silver jewelry are handpicked. Well stocked without being overwhelming. (416-979-1992; 14 Kensington Ave; 11am-6pm Mon-Sat, 1-5pm Sun; 505, 510)

Sonic Boom
MUSIC

20 MAP P94, D5

The largest indie record store in Canada, Sonic Boom has rows upon rows of new and used vinyl, CDs and even cassettes. Long-time staffers are deeply knowledgeable, offering direction and advice. Quirky T-shirts, irreverent souvenirs and coffee-table books (most with a musical bent) are sold at the front. (📞416-532-0334; https://sonicboommusic.com; 215 Spadina Ave; ⏰10am-10pm; 🚌310, 510)

Bungalow   VINTAGE
21 🔒 MAP P94, B2

A vintage store selling well-curated home goods, furniture and clothing. Items change regularly, but expect mid-century Modern tableware, teak bowls and trays, retro sunglasses and pillbox hats. New hipster clothing and accessories also sold. (📞416-598-0204; www.bungalow.to; 273 Augusta Ave; ⏰11am-6:30pm Mon-Thu, to 8pm Fri & Sat, to 6pm Sun; 🚌306, 506)

Bay of Spirits Gallery   GIFTS & SOUVENIRS
22 🔒 MAP P94, F4

The works of Norval Morrisseau – the first indigenous artist to have a solo exhibit at the **National Gallery of Canada** (www.gallery.ca) – are proudly on display in this atmospheric space, which carries aboriginal art from across the country. Look for the Pacific West Coast totem poles (from miniature to over 4m tall), Inuit carvings and Inukshuk figurines. (📞416-971-5190; www.bayofspirits.com; 334 Dundas St W; ⏰10am-5pm Tue-Sat, noon-5pm Sun; 🚌505)

Vintage clothes, Kensington Market

MEC   SPORTS & OUTDOORS
23 🔒 MAP P94, E6

MEC is your mecca if you have a fetish for outdoor and adventure equipment. Multiple brands of backpacking, camping, hiking and travel gear line the walls of this Canadian storehouse; sign up for lifetime membership ($5) on the spot to make a purchase. The helpful staff are swamped on weekends, so try midweek if you need advice. (Mountain Equipment Co-op; 📞416-340-2667; www.mec.ca; 300 Queen St W; ⏰10am-9pm Mon-Fri, 9am-8pm Sat, 10am-6pm Sun; 📶; Ⓢ Osgoode)

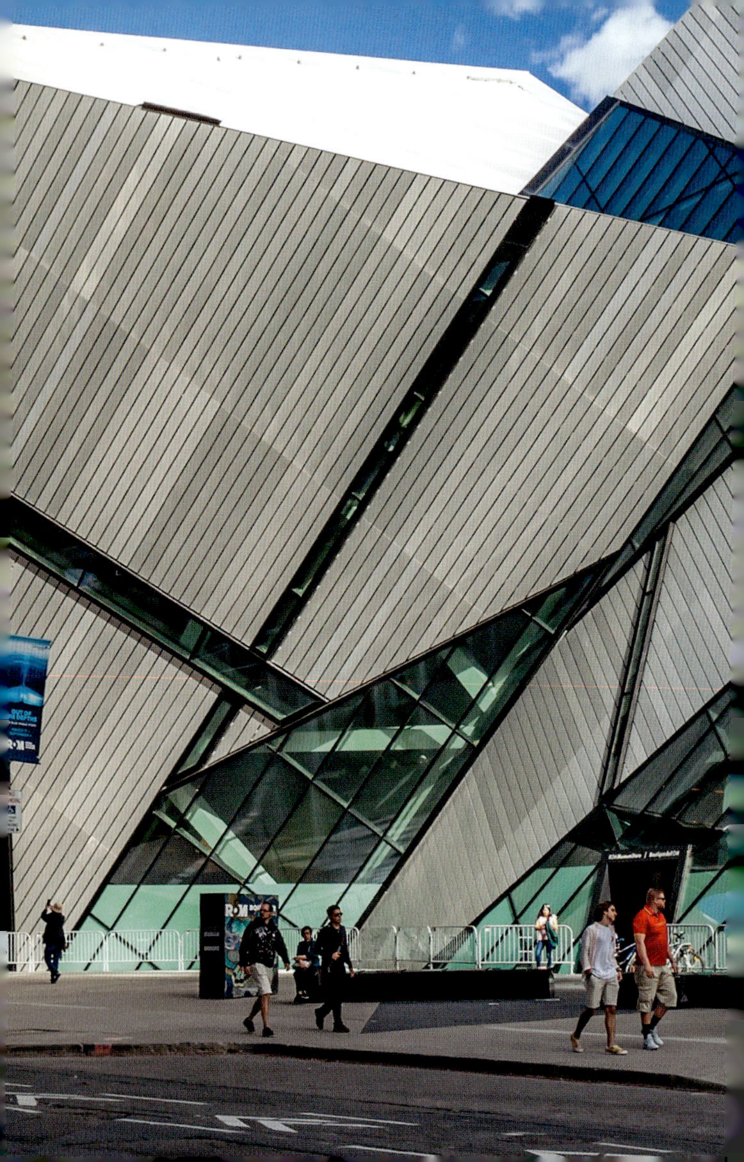

Explore
Yorkville & the Annex

This a district of odd bedfellows, from Yorkville's four-star hotels, luxe shopping and homes of the fabulous at the eastern end to the Annex's gritty streets, world eats and downtown residential area – the city's largest, favored by students and academics – at the western end. The students are from the prestigious University of Toronto, which forms the neighborhood's southern edge with its stately Victorian and Romanesque buildings. Nearby is the city's finest natural-history museum, as well as several other worthwhile museums.

The Short List

- **Royal Ontario Museum (p104)** Getting lost in Canada's largest and most extensive museum of natural history and world culture.

- **Hot Docs (p114)** Catching a couple of docs (or a couple of dozen) at the largest documentary festival in North America.

- **Mink Mile (p115)** Feasting your eyes on the boutiques and luxury stores in this sumptuous district, Toronto's answer to NYC's Fifth Ave.

- **Bata Shoe Museum (p108)** Marveling at the thousands of shoes and related items, some more than 4000 years old.

Getting There & Around

- M The Green line has several stops along Bloor St.
- 🚌 The 94A runs east–west across the district on Wellesley St/Harbord St.

Neighborhood Map on p106

Royal Ontario Museum (p104)
JHVEPHOTO/SHUTTERSTOCK ©; ARCHITECT: DANIEL LIBESKIND

Top Sight
Royal Ontario Museum

One of the largest museums in North America, the ROM dazzles with gallery upon gallery of fossils, artifacts and art, as well as hands-on exhibits and weekly events. The building itself is fascinating: an amalgam of old and new. Come here for a day or a week – you'll likely always have more to see. Docent-led tours help unpack the place.

◎ MAP P106, E3

ROM

www.rom.on.ca

100 Queen's Park

adult/child $23/14, 5:30-8:30pm 3rd Mon of month free

⊙ 10am-5:30pm daily, to 8:30pm 3rd Mon of month

Ⓢ Museum

First Peoples Art & Culture Gallery

This gallery provides insight into the works of art and cultural heritage of Canada's indigenous people from precolonial times to the present. The collection includes ceremonial clothing, birch-bark canoes, fine art and more. A small theater screens documentaries and hosts live performances, adding a present-day perspective to the collection. Knowledgeable staffers are available on weekdays to answer questions.

Hands-On Galleries

Younger visitors will appreciate ROM's two interactive galleries: the **Discovery Gallery** and the **Family Gallery of Hands-on Biodiversity**. Kids can touch shark skulls and beaver pelts, dig for dinosaur bones and walk through bat caves. Imaginative play has children hiding in foxholes and dressing up as medieval folk. Facilitators share what's on offer and answer the many questions kids have.

Mosaic Ceiling

Though ROM is filled with a dizzying number of artifacts and art, its mosaic ceiling itself is dazzling. Commissioned in 1933 by the museum's first director, the ceiling is made up of over a million Venetian tiles in myriad patterns and symbols representing the breadth of ROM's collection. Look for the Mayan temple, the Egyptian falcon, the three-clawed Chinese dragon, the bison and more.

Don't Miss

- Prehistoric skeletons in the Gallery of the Age of Mammals
- Colonial art in the Gallery of Canada
- Ceremonial masks in the Gallery of Africa, The Americas, and Asia-Pacific
- The Bat Cave

★ Top Tips

- Admission is free the third Monday evening of the month – arrive after 6pm to avoid the rush.
- Audio tours to select galleries can be downloaded from the website.
- Docent-led tours are offered daily in English and French.
- Strollers are available for rent at the coat check.
- Special exhibits are often excellent but cost extra.

✘ Take a Break

Druxy's ROM Café, the museum's basement-level cafeteria, offers burgers, sandwiches, pizza, drinks and more.

If you're looking for something a little more flash, head to nearby Trattoria Nervosa (p112) for patio dining near the Mink Mile.

Yorkville & the Annex

106

For reviews see

- ◉ Top Sights — p104
- ◎ Sights — p108
- ⊗ Eating — p110
- 🍸 Drinking — p112
- ★ Entertainment — p113
- 🔒 Shopping — p115

Native Canadian Centre of Toronto

Bata Shoe Museum

THE ANNEX

KENSINGTON MARKET

TIFF Bell Lightbox (1.4km)

107

Yorkville & the Annex

YORKVILLE

Royal Ontario Museum

Gardiner Museum

Map labels:
- Tranby Ave
- Boswell Ave
- Elgin Ave
- Bedford Road
- Hazelton Ave
- Church St
- Scollard St
- Yorkville Ave
- Collier St
- Prince Arthur Ave
- Avenue Rd
- Bellair St
- Bay St
- Yonge St
- Asquith Ave
- Cumberland St
- Bay
- Bloor-Yonge
- Bloor St W
- Bloor St E
- St Thomas St
- Balmuto St
- Hayden St
- ROMbus
- Museum
- Charles St W
- St Mary St
- **YONGE ST STRIP**
- Isabella St
- Varsity Stadium
- Hoskin Ave
- Queen's Park Cres W
- Queen's Park Cres E
- Queen's Park
- Irwin Ave
- Gloucester St
- St Joseph St
- Dundonald St
- Phipps St
- St Nicholas St
- Wellesley
- Wellesley St W
- Wellesley St E
- Tower Rd
- University of Toronto (St George Campus)
- Breadalbane St
- Maitland St
- Bay St
- Alexander St
- Grosvenor St
- Grenville St
- Wood St
- Queens Park
- College St
- College
- Carlton St
- King's College Rd
- McCaul St
- Orde St
- University Ave
- Toronto General Hospital
- Elizabeth St
- LaPlante Ave
- Heritage Toronto (1.7km)
- Barbara Ann Scott Park

Scale: 500 m / 0.25 miles

Markers: 1, 2, 5, 13, 16, 17, 22, 23, 25

Sights

Bata Shoe Museum — MUSEUM

1 ◎ MAP P106, D2

It's important in life to be well shod, a stance the Bata Shoe Museum takes seriously. Impressively designed by Raymond Moriyama to resemble a stylized shoebox, the museum houses a collection of 13,000 'pedi-artifacts' from around the globe, spanning 4500 years; only 3% to 4% are on view at any given time. Peruse 19th-century French chestnut-crushing clogs, Canadian aboriginal polar boots or famous modern pairs worn by Elton John, Indira Gandhi and Pablo Picasso. Come along for something truly different. (☎ 416-979-7799; www.batashoemuseum.ca; 327 Bloor St W; adult/child $14/5, 5-8pm Thu suggested donation $5; ⌚10am-5pm Mon-Wed, Fri & Sat, to 8pm Thu, noon-5pm Sun; Ⓢ St George)

Gardiner Museum — MUSEUM

2 ◎ MAP P106, F3

Opposite the Royal Ontario Museum (p104), the Gardiner was founded by philanthropists to house their ceramics. Spread over three floors, the collections cover several millennia; various rooms focus on 17th- and 18th-century English tavern ware, Italian Renaissance majolica, ancient American earthenware and blue-and-white Chinese porcelain. Check the website for special exhibits. Free guided tours daily at 2pm.

Toronto's Artifacts

The oldest human artifact found in Toronto is a 10,000-year-old arrowhead, or Holcombe point, found in the present-day Forest Hill neighborhood. See it and many of the city's other archaeological discoveries at the **Royal Ontario Museum** (p104).

(☎ 416-586-8080; www.gardinermuseum.on.ca; 111 Queen's Park; adult/child $15/free, 4-9pm Wed half-price; ⌚10am-6pm Mon, Tue, Thu & Fri, to 9pm Wed, to 5pm Sat & Sun; Ⓢ Museum)

Casa Loma — HISTORIC BUILDING

3 ◎ MAP P106, C1

Toronto's only castle may never have housed royalty, but it certainly has grandeur, lording over the Annex from a cliff that was once the shoreline of the glacial Lake Iroquois, from which Lake Ontario derived. A self-guided audio tour leads visitors through the four levels of the Edwardian mansion as well as the 800ft tunnel to the stables; the top floor houses a military museum. Head to the pool turned theater first, where a short film provides a good overview. (☎ 416-923-1171; www.casaloma.org; 1 Austin Tce; adult/child $33/23; ⌚9:30am-5pm, last entry 4pm; Ⓟ; 🚌127, Ⓢ Dupont)

Spadina Museum
MUSEUM

4 ⊙ MAP P106, C1

Atop the Baldwin Steps, this gracious home and its Victorian-Edwardian gardens were built in 1866 as a country estate for financier James Austin and his family. Donated to the city in 1978, it became a museum in 1984 and was painstakingly transformed to evoke the heady age of the 1920s and '30s. Knowledgeable guides lead visitors through the estate, sharing the history of the home and the Austin family along the way – highly recommended. (📞416-392-6910; www.toronto.ca/museums; 285 Spadina Rd; tours adult/child $10/6, grounds free; ⊙noon-5pm Tue-Sun Apr-Aug, noon-4pm Mon-Fri, to 5pm Sat & Sun Sep-Dec; 🅿; Ⓢ Dupont)

ROMBus
BUS

5 ⊙ MAP P106, F3

Toronto's Royal Ontario Museum (p104) organizes occasional special tours, with educated and enthusiastic guides, around historical, cultural and architectural themes. Full-day tours are either in town or within a couple of hours of it. Although they're pricey, the tours are well worth it if they pique your interest. (📞416-586-8000; www.rom.on.ca/en/whats-on/rombus; 100 Queen's Park; full-day tours $135-145; Ⓢ Museum)

Vintage shoes, Bata Shoe Museum

Native Canadian Centre of Toronto
CULTURAL

6 ⊙ MAP P106, C2

This community center hosts Thursday-night drum socials, seasonal powwows and elders' cultural events that promote harmony and conversation between tribal members and non-indigenous people. You can also sign up for workshops and craft classes, such as beading and dancing. A gift shop sells handcrafted items, including jewelry, moccasins and T-shirts. (NCCT; 📞416-964-9087; www.ncct.on.ca; 16 Spadina Rd; ⊙9am-8pm Mon-Wed, to 9pm Thu, to 6pm Fri, 10am-4pm Sat; Ⓢ Spadina)

Eating

Aunties & Uncles　　　CAFE $

7 ✕ MAP P106, A6

There's usually a line on the sidewalk outside the picket fence of this always-bustling brunch/lunch joint with a simple menu of cheap-and-cheery homemade favorites. Plop yourself down in one of the mismatched chairs and dig into dishes like grilled Brie with pear chutney and walnuts on challah, banana-oatmeal pancakes or grilled Canadian cheddar. Cash only. (☏416-324-1375; www.auntiesanduncles.ca; 74 Lippincott St; mains $8-10; ⏲9am-3pm; 🚌510)

Annex Food Hall　　　FOOD HALL $

8 ✕ MAP P106, B2

Find some of the best tasty, quick eats at this industrial-chic food hall: vegan bowls, steamed-bun sandwiches, fried chicken, Bangkok-style street food, tacos and more. Order at individual counters and grab a seat at a communal picnic table. Popular with the budget-minded, especially University of Toronto students. (www.theannexfoodhall.com; 384 Bloor St W; mains $6-14; ⏲11:30am-9pm Sun-Wed, to 10pm Thu-Sat; Ⓢ Spadina)

Harbord Bakery　　　BAKERY $

9 ✕ MAP P106, B4

A Toronto institution, this Jewish bakery has been serving customers since 1945. Stocked with all sorts of pies, cakes, cookies and bread, the challah and butter tarts are considered among the best in town. If you're hankering for a meal, check out the small prepared-foods section, with salads, sandwiches, mains...even matzo-ball soup! (☏416-922-5767; www.harbordbakery.ca; 115 Harbord St; from $2.75; ⏲8am-7pm Mon-Thu, to 6pm Fri & Sat, to 4pm Sun; 🚌310, 510)

Fuwa Fuwa　　　JAPANESE $

10 ✕ MAP P106, B2

Meaning 'Fluffy, Fluffy,' Fuwa Fuwa specializes in Japanese soufflé pancakes. Traditionally served after weddings as a sign of good fortune, here they're served daily in a small, bright-yellow eatery. The pancakes themselves are light and airy and come topped with sweet treats like tiramisu cream

---

Walking Tours

Heritage Toronto (☏416-338-3886; www.heritagetoronto.org; 157 King St E; suggested donation $10; ⏲May-Oct) offers fascinating historical, cultural and nature walks, as well as bus (TTC) tours, led by museum experts, neighborhood historical-society members and emerging historians. Tours generally last one to three hours. Check the website for a handful of downloadable self-guided tours, too.

and coffee syrup or crème brûlée sauce and vanilla ice cream. A good dessert-for-dinner option. (☎ 647-618-2868; www.fuwafuwapancakes.com; 408 Bloor St W; mains $11-16; ⏰ 11am-10pm Mon-Thu, to 11pm Fri, 10am-11pm Sat, to 10pm Sun; 🚇 Bathurst)

Sushi on Bloor SUSHI $

11 ✖ MAP P106, A2

Among the countless sushi restaurants on Bloor, this one stands out, its wooden booths and long tables always packed with customers enjoying platters of high-quality sushi at decent prices. Bento boxes are available, too. Great daily specials, starting at just $5, often include miso soup and salad. (☎ 416-516-3456; www.sushionbloor.com; 525 Bloor St W; rolls from $5.50, meals from $12; ⏰ 11:30am-11:30pm Mon-Thu, to midnight Fri, noon-midnight Sat, to 10pm Sun; 🚇 Bathurst)

Mr Tonkatsu JAPANESE $

12 ✖ MAP P106, A2

Asking you to grind up your own sesame-seed rice topping might just be a trick to show you how authentic this place is, but it works. The crumbed pork (or chicken) is properly crispy outside and juicy inside, and Mr Tonkatsu has that nice-but-casual vibe you find in restaurants all over Japan. (☎ 416-537-9000; www.mrtonkatsu.com; 530 Bloor St W; mains $12-16; ⏰ 11:30am-2:30pm & 4:30-10pm Mon-Sat, to 9pm Sun; 🚇 Bathurst)

Japanese soufflé pancakes at Fuwa Fuwa

Trattoria Nervosa ITALIAN $$

13 MAP P106, G2

In the heart of fancy Yorkville, this restaurant is an attitude-free oasis. The patio is a good corner from which to people watch well-heeled passersby while you dig into simple, excellent pasta – the *mafalde ai funghi* has incredibly deep mushroom flavors without being overly creamy. (416-961-4642; www.eatnervosa.com; 75 Yorkville Ave; mains $17-33; 11:30am-10pm Mon-Wed, to 11pm Thu-Sat, noon-10pm Sun; Bay)

Piano Piano ITALIAN $$

14 MAP P106, C4

Meaning 'slowly, slowly' in Italian, Piano Piano is all about slowing down to enjoy a meal and connect with friends and family. The menu itself is traditional Italian – smoked burrata, freshly made ravioli, bone-in veal Parmesan, roasted-mushroom pizza – with plenty of vegan and gluten-free options. If you're coming with a group, ask about the 'family-style' menu. (416-929-7788; www.pianopianotherestaurant.com; 88 Harbord St; mains $18-29; noon-3pm & 5-10pm Sun-Wed, to 11pm Thu-Sat; 310, 510)

Café Cancan FRENCH $$

15 MAP P106, B4

This bistro is a pastel dream, with baby-pink walls, teal banquette seating and hints of yellow. The patio is just as elegant, and the food just as divine. The menu includes classics such as escargot and foie gras, or you can enjoy eggs Benedict or a burger at brunch or dinner. Snap a photo by the iconic pink door. (647-341-3100; www.cafecancan.com; 89 Harbord St; mains $18-28; 11am-3pm & 6-10pm Mon-Fri, 10am-3pm & 5-10pm Sat & Sun; 310, 510)

Sassafraz FUSION $$$

16 MAP P106, G2

Popular with visiting celebrities and a moneyed clientele, Sassafraz epitomizes Yorkville with its elegant yet breezy decor. Jazz combos serenade weekend brunchers, and sassy receptionists distribute diners between the sun-drenched patio and the leafy indoor courtyard. The food? Predictably good. Dress to impress. (416-964-2222; www.sassafraz.ca; 100 Cumberland St; mains $22-29; 11:30am-11pm Mon-Thu, to 1am Fri, 11am-1pm Sat, to 11pm Sun; Bay)

Drinking

Oxley PUB

17 MAP P106, F2

A first-class British pub, the Oxley is located in a 19th-century row house in the heart of Yorkville. Two floors of leather seating, ornate wallpaper and Victorian-era decor fill with business folk and the well-heeled hankering for a 20oz pour of craft beer, a glass of wine or a stiff drink. Classic English fare served, too. (☎647-348-1300; https://theoxley.com; 121 Yorkville Ave; ⏰11:30am-midnight Mon-Wed, to 1am Thu, to 2am Fri, 10am-2am Sat, to midnight Sun; 📶; Ⓢ Bay)

Slanted Door COFFEE
18 🚇 MAP P106, A2

A bright, contemporary coffee shop, the Slanted Door doubles as a gallery, showcasing work by emerging artists on its walls upstairs and down. The coffee drinks and teas are strong and flavorful, and the smoothies creative, with combos like apple-ginger-beet. Light snacks available, too. This is a popular place to catch up with friends or emails. (☎647-358-9888; https://slanteddoor.ca; 442 Bloor St W; ⏰8:30am-7:30pm Mon-Fri, 9am-6:30pm Sat, 10am-5:30pm; 📶; Ⓢ Bathurst)

Madison Avenue Pub PUB
19 🚇 MAP P106, C2

Comprising three Victorian houses in the Annex, the rowdy 'Maddy' draws a late-20s University of Toronto crowd. There are billiards, darts, a sports bar, polished brass, antique-y lamps lighting the curtained upper floors, *five* patios and lots of hormones colliding. (☎416-927-1722; www.madisonavenuepub.com; 14-18 Madison Ave; ⏰11am-2am Mon-Sat, to midnight Sun; Ⓢ Spadina)

Entertainment

Hot Docs Ted Rogers Cinema CINEMA
20 ⭐ MAP P106, A2

This art deco theater with a two-tiered balcony screens a wonderfully varied schedule of new releases, art-house flicks, shorts, documentaries and vintage films,

---

Local Experiences

Drinking
○ In Yorkville, the **Oxley** is the go-to spot for after-work drinks.

Shopping
○ Join the well-heeled on Yorkville Ave, a couple of blocks from the Mink Mile, to shop for luxury items at well-respected boutiques such as **Pink Tartan** (p115).

Eating
○ Though sushi restaurants are a dime a dozen in The Annex, U of T students keep **Sushi on Bloor** (p111) packed most nights.

Hollywood North

'Hollywood North' is a name claimed by both Toronto and Vancouver. Historically, Vancouver has rights to the title – it began hosting film productions in 1910, emerging in the 1970s as a desirable alternative to LA for shooting films and TV programs, complete with tax breaks and cheaper labor. Toronto jumped into the game in the 1970s too, but it was not until the 2000s that it really came into its own. Toronto aggressively courted big-budget productions, offering generous tax incentives (some say too generous) for using local services.

It proved a great place to shoot film and TV. It has a deep and diverse pool of local acting talent; innumerable set locations, from modern cityscapes to historic buildings; and world-class production facilities, like Pinewood Toronto, which has more than 23,000 sq meters of production space and North America's largest custom sound studio. Financially, Toronto recorded over $1.25 billion in production activity in 2011, surpassing Vancouver for the first time; by 2018 the figure was over $2 billion.

Of course, for visitors, watching films are the priority. For that, Toronto has no shortage of options. Beyond regular cinemas, Toronto hosts dozens of film-related events, most notably the **Toronto International Film Festival** (TIFF; 888-599-8433; www.tiff.net; 504), held yearly in September. It's headquartered at the **TIFF Bell Lightbox** (p55) with screenings – more than 300 in all – held at venues throughout the city. There's also **Hot Docs** (Canadian International Documentary Festival; 416-637-3123; www.hotdocs.ca; 506 Bloor St W; from $17.50; late Apr-early May; Bathurst), North America's largest documentary film festival, with more than 200 screenings held in April and May, mostly at the beautifully restored **Hot Docs Ted Rogers Cinema** (p113). And there are also many smaller niche festivals, such as LGBTIQ+ film festival **Inside Out** (Toronto LGBT Film Festival; 416-977-6847; www.insideout.ca; 350 King St W; tickets from $48; late May–early Jun; 504), and imagiNATIVE, which showcases international and Canadian indigenous filmmakers and artists.

Curious about the films made in Toronto? Big hits include:

- *The Shape of Water* (2017)
- *Spotlight* (2015)
- *Mean Girls* (2004)
- *My Big Fat Greek Wedding* (2002)
- *Good Will Hunting* (1997)

and is home to the mind-expanding Hot Docs (p114) international documentary festival. (Bloor Hot Docs Cinema; ☎416-637-3123; http://hotdocscinema.ca; 506 Bloor St W; Ⓢ Bathurst)

Lee's Palace LIVE MUSIC

21 ⭐ MAP P106, A2

Legendary Lee's Palace has set the stage over the years for Dinosaur Jr, the Smashing Pumpkins and Queens of the Stone Age. Kurt Cobain started an infamous bottle-throwing incident when Nirvana played here in 1990. You can't miss it – look for the primary-colored mural that seems to scream out front. (☎416-532-1598; www.leespalace.com; 529 Bloor St W; ⏱8pm-2:30am; Ⓢ Bathurst)

Shopping

Mink Mile FASHION & ACCESSORIES

22 🛍 MAP P106, G2

Often compared to NYC's Fifth Ave, Toronto's Mink Mile is home to well-known luxury stores such as Tiffany & Co, Prada, Hermès, Louis Vuitton and more. Nowhere near a mile long – it's only about 600m – it's distinguishable by its granite sidewalks, public art and mature trees. Come here to walk among the uber-wealthy or pick up some designer duds. (Bloor St W, btwn Yonge St & Avenue Rd; ⏱most shops 10am-7pm; Ⓢ Bay, Bloor-Yonge)

Pink Tartan FASHION & ACCESSORIES

23 🛍 MAP P106, G2

Chic Pink Tartan boutique sells designer clothing and accessories with a preppy bent. It's housed in a gorgeous historic building, built for Yorkville's constable in the mid-1800s. A go-to for Toronto's upper crust. (☎416-516-0641; https://pinktartan.ca; 77 Yorkville Ave; ⏱11am-6pm Mon-Thu, to 7pm Fri & Sat, noon-5pm Sun; Ⓢ Bay)

BMV BOOKS

24 🛍 MAP P106, B2

The biggest (and most popular) used bookstore in Toronto, with a spectacular selection of titles. Vinyls and DVDs sold, too. It has a smaller second location on Dundas Sq. (☎416-967-5757; www.bmvbooks.com; 471 Bloor St W; ⏱10am-11pm Mon-Wed, to midnight Thu-Sat, noon-9pm Sun; Ⓢ Spadina)

Page & Panel: The TCAF Shop COMICS

25 🛍 MAP P106, H2

What started as a pop-up for the Toronto Comic Arts Festival (TCAF) has become a permanent comics hub. It's a well-curated store, with excellent picks of Canadian and international graphic novels and designer gifts. (☎416-323-9212; www.torontocomics.com/tcafshop; 789 Yonge St; ⏱10:30am-8:30pm Mon-Fri, to 5pm Sat, noon-5pm Sun; Ⓢ Bloor-Yonge)

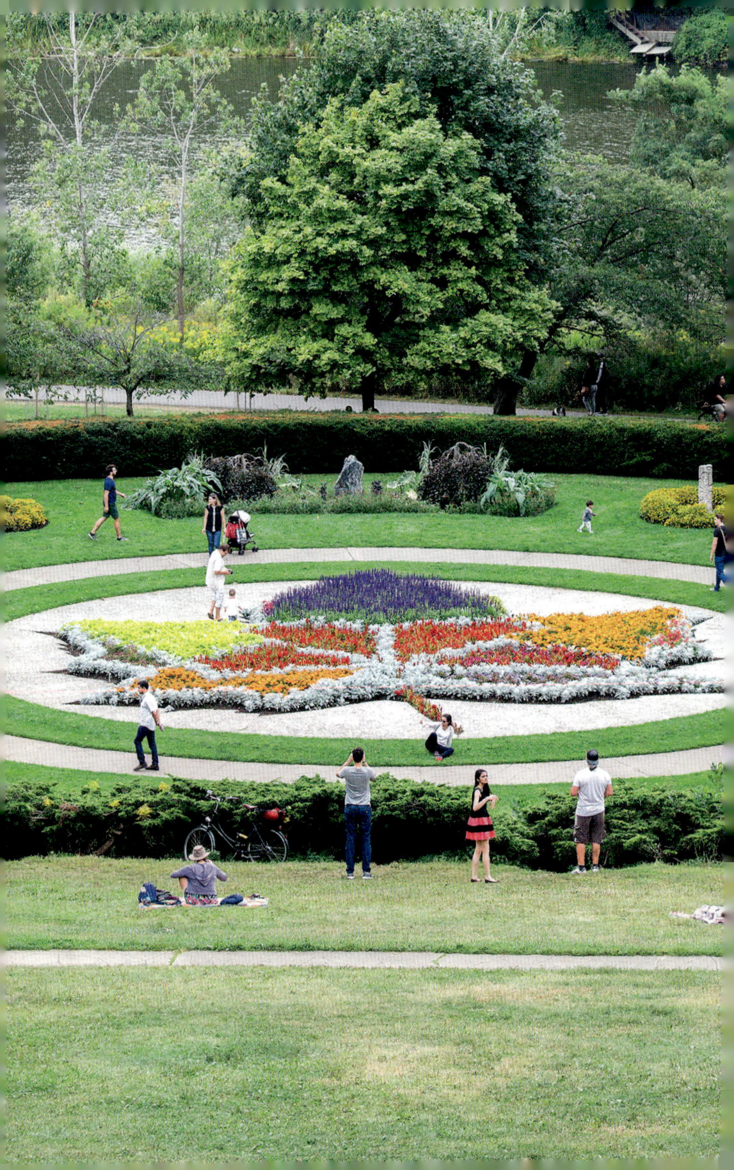

Explore
West End

For many, the West End is quintessential hipster Toronto, where the city's rich diversity, artfulness, grit and cosmopolitan flair are on full display. You'll find terrific shopping and trendy bars on Queen St W, venerable Italian and Portuguese enclaves along College St, and the rolling expanse of High Park, one of the city's finest urban green spaces.

The Short List

- ***Shopping (p128)*** *Finding something along Queen St W for everyone on your list, whether it's folk art, cheeky tees or specialty snacks.*

- ***Nightlife (p125)*** *Dancing to live bands and top DJs or sipping cocktails on the Drake Hotel's sweet rooftop patio.*

- ***Arts (p125)*** *Rubbing shoulders with working artists, who enjoy studio, gallery and performance space at the Gladstone.*

- ***High Park (p118)*** *Relaxing in Torontonians' favorite park, where you can cycle beneath the cherry blossoms, go ice skating or take a guided nature walk.*

- ***Museum of Contemporary Art Toronto (p122)*** *Pondering the meaning of contemporary art, installed in a repurposed aluminum factory.*

Getting There & Around

[M] The Green line has several stations along Bloor St in the West End.

Streetcar The 501 runs along Queen St W from East Toronto; the 506 runs along College St to High Park.

Neighborhood Map on p120

Maple Leaf Garden, High Park (p118) MANU M NAIR/SHUTTERSTOCK ©

Top Sight
High Park

A favorite among locals, High Park is a verdant, forested expanse with trails, gardens, cherry-tree groves, loads of kid-friendly areas...even outdoor theater productions! The Nature Centre, the hub of organized activities, offers guided walks and interesting events. An engaging and beautiful place, the park showcases another side of the West End.

◉ MAP P120, A1

www.toronto.ca/parks

1873 Bloor St W

⊘ dawn-dusk

P 👤

S High Park, 🚋 501, 506, 508

Nature Centre

High Park's Nature Centre offers rich programming for children and adults, including workshops and speaker series. A highlight is the guided **family nature walks**, led by experienced naturalists. Walks have various themes – Moth Nights, Oaks in the Urban Savannah, Wild Bees – but all integrate information about the park's ecosystems and flora and fauna. Walks are by donation and usually last two hours. Even if you don't attend a workshop or join a walk, it's worth stopping by the center to get the lay of the land.

Ponds & Creeks

High Park is dotted and lined with ponds and creeks – perfect for exploring and spotting wildlife. The largest, Grenadier Pond, is a great place to see **waterbirds** such as white egrets and trumpeter swans. In winter the pond is used as an ice-skating rink.

Shakespeare in High Park

Shakespeare in High Park (416-368-3110; www.canadianstage.com; suggested donation adult/child $20/free; 8pm Tue-Sun Jul-Sep), pictured left, is one of Canada's longest-running outdoor theater events, having started in 1982. Guests sit on grassy levels by the amphitheater or – if they pay a little extra and in advance – on a cushion in a premium area near the stage. Bring a blanket and a picnic dinner to enjoy the show like a local.

Don't Miss...

- Shakespeare in High Park
- Guided nature walks
- Cherry blossoms in spring
- Ice skating on Grenadier Pond
- Train rides through the park

★ Top Tips

- If you're visiting in late April or early May, be sure to check out the park's cherry blossoms. The main grove is between Grenadier Café and Grenadier Pond, with more at the Maple Leaf Garden and along West Rd.

- Though tickets to Shakespeare in High Park are by suggested donation, if you pay a set $30 per ticket online you'll score a padded seat near the stage.

- Hillside Gardens is a great place for photos, with small paths, fountains and what seems like an endless display of flowers.

✕ Take a Break

In the heart of the park, **Grenadier Café** makes a welcome pit stop, especially if you stick to basics like burgers and sandwiches; takeout service is offered, too.

For more (and better) options, head to nearby Queen St W and Grand Electric Parkdale (p122), with its hipster vibe and delicious tacos.

West End

For reviews see
- Top Sights — p118
- Sights — p122
- Eating — p122
- Drinking — p124
- Entertainment — p127
- Shopping — p128

High Park

Museum of Contemporary Art Toronto 1

Dundas W
Lansdowne
Dufferin
Bloor St W

Croatia St
Dufferin St
Dufferin Grove Park
Havelock St

Lansdowne Ave
St Clarens Ave
Marguaretta St
Brock Ave
Sterling Rd
Lynd Ave 6

BROCKTON VILLAGE
Muir Ave
Lindsey Ave

Grenadier Rd
College St
Dundas St W

Wabash Ave
Shirley St
Wright Ave
Fern Ave
Garden Ave
Galley Ave
Pearson Ave

Sheridan Ave

LITTLE PORTUGAL

Triller Ave
Sorauren Ave
Macdonell Ave
Lansdowne Ave
Brock Ave
Dufferin St
Gladstone Ave

PARKDALE

Queen St W 29 4 27   14
                            18
                 30
              24

Dowling Ave
Jameson Ave
Close Ave
Dunn Ave
Cowan Ave
Elm Grove Ave
Gwynne Ave

Gardiner Expwy
King St W

West End

121

Map Grid References

Row 1 (E–H)
- Northumberland St
- Ossington (S)
- Christie Pitts Park
- Christie St
- Barton Ave
- Christie (S)
- London St
- 19 Bathurst (S)
- Bloor St W
- 5, 3

Row 2
- 22
- Lennox St
- Hepbourne St
- Dovercourt Rd
- Delaware Ave
- Concord Ave
- Ossington Ave
- Roxton Rd
- Shaw St
- Crawford St
- Bickford Park
- Page St
- Clinton St
- Manning Ave
- Euclid Ave
- Palmerston Blvd
- Markham St
- Harbord St
- Harbord Park
- Jersey Ave
- Ulster St
- Dewson St

Row 3
- Dewson St
- Montrose Ave
- Beatrice St
- Grace St
- 23
- LITTLE ITALY
- 8
- College St
- Shannon St
- 12

Row 4
- Henderson Ave
- Lakeview Ave
- Harrison St
- Shaw St
- Crawford St
- Montrose Ave
- Beatrice St
- Grace St
- 20
- TRINITY-BELLWOODS
- Dundas St W
- Bathurst St

Row 5
- Rolyat St
- 7
- 10
- Foxley St
- 13
- Argyle St
- 11
- Humbert St
- 9
- Bruce St
- Rebecca St
- 16
- Trinity Bellwoods Park
- Lobb Ave
- Trinity Dr
- Gore Valley Ave
- Bellwoods Ave
- Claremont St
- Manning Ave
- Euclid Ave
- Palmerston Ave
- Markham St
- Robinson St
- Logie Pl
- Crocker Ave
- Queen St W
- 25
- 28 Willis St

Row 6
- 21, 2
- WEST QUEEN WEST
- 26
- Massey St
- Strachan Ave
- Stafford St
- Niagara St
- Richmond St W
- Mitchell Ave
- Tesameth St
- Sudbury St
- Shank St
- Stanley Park
- King St W

Sights

Museum of Contemporary Art Toronto
MUSEUM

1 MAP P120, B2

Housed in what was once Toronto's tallest building – a factory producing aluminum parts – MOCA exhibits innovative works by Canadian and international artists that address themes of contemporary relevance. Exhibits change four times per year, but all seek to provoke and engage viewers, whether they like what they see or not. (MOCA Toronto; 416-530-2500; http://museumofcontemporaryart.ca; 158 Sterling Rd; adult/child $10/free, 10am-2pm last Sun of month free; 10am-5pm Wed-Mon, to 9pm Fri; P; S Lansdowne, 306, 506)

Eating

Otto's Bierhalle
GERMAN $

2 MAP P120, E6

Garage doors, long communal tables, a wide selection of draft beers and ciders, huge platters of brats and schnitzels – it looks like Oktoberfest pretty much year-round here (the only thing missing is the oompah band). A popular spot with an upbeat vibe, this place makes out-of-towners feel like part of the city. Reservations recommended on weekends. (416-901-5472; www.ottosbierhalle.com; 1087 Queen St W; mains $10-16; noon-11pm Mon & Tue, to midnight Wed & Thu, to 2am Sat, to 10pm Sun; 501)

Los Guaca-Moles
MEXICAN $

3 MAP P120, G1

Tucked just off Bloor St, Guaca-Moles serves authentic Mexican dishes in a black-painted converted brick house. Choose from classics like *elote* (Mexican street corn), enchiladas, *moles* and so many taco varieties it'll be tough (there's even cactus and hibiscus flower!). Drinks include *aguas frescas* (water-based fruit drinks) and, of course, margaritas. Be sure to save room for the churros. (647-347-5031; www.losguaca-moles.ca; 690 Euclid Ave; mains $9-18; 5-10:30pm Tue-Thu, to 11:30pm Fri & Sat, 3-10pm Sun; S Christie)

Grand Electric Parkdale
MEXICAN $

4 MAP P120, C5

Got a craving for tacos? This hip Mexican joint in the West End serves up some of the best in the city, and the wings are pretty darn awesome, too. There's limited seating, so prepare to wait in line for a table; in summer, try to snag one on the gorgeous backyard patio. (416-627-3459; http://grandelectrictoronto.com; 1330 Queen St W; tacos $5, mains $12-14; noon-11pm Sun-Thu, noon-midnight Fri & Sat; 501)

NishDish
NATIVE AMERICAN $

5 MAP P120, G1

Traditional Anishnawbe (Nish) dishes are served at this tiny eatery – more a quick-service counter than a cafe – with two long communal tables. The menu changes weekly, but expect game, beans, and regional fruits and veggies; eg hominy-corn soup, boar omelet, elk chili, wild-rice blueberry pudding and, of course, fry bread. Service is friendly: if in doubt, just ask. (416-855-4085; www.nishdish.com; 690 Bloor St W; mains $7-14; 10am-7pm Mon-Fri, 9am-6pm Sat & Sun; S Christie)

Commoner GASTROPUB $$
6 MAP P120, A3

The Commoner is a swanky gastropub in Roncesvalles Village. Lush jewel tones and antique pieces fill the massive yet welcoming space, and the patio is great for sipping craft beer or cocktails on warm summer days. Stop by for dinner during the week or brunch on the weekend. Either way, try the buffalo cauliflower. (647-351-2067; www.thecommonerrestaurant.ca; 2067 Dundas St W; mains $13-27; 5-11pm Mon-Thu, to midnight Fri, 11am-midnight Sat, to 11pm Sun; 506)

Pizzeria Libretto ITALIAN $$
7 MAP P120, F4

Pizza Libretto crafts what is arguably the best pizza in town. The secret? A wood-fired oven built by a third-generation pizza-oven builder with stones shipped from Italy. Besides certified Neapolitan pizza and other Naples staples, the menu includes a prix-fixe weekday lunch (salad, pizza and gelato for $16) and an all-Italian wine list. Vegan cheese and gluten-free dough available. (416-532-8000; http://pizzerialibretto.com; 221 Ossington Ave; mains $15-25; 11:30am-10pm Mon-Wed, to 11pm Thu-Sun; 505)

DaiLo CHINESE $$
8 MAP P120, H3

Not your typical Chinese restaurant, this chic Asian brasserie is embellished with teal and gold and serves up Little-Italy-does-French-inspired-Chinese dishes. From the fried watermelon to the jackfruit and chili-glazed back ribs, you'll want to try every single thing on the menu. (647-341-8882; http://dailoto.com; 503 College St; mains $14-48; 5:30-11pm Tue-Sun; 506)

Best in the West

If you like to eat, eat well, and eat at the hottest tickets in town, this is where it's at. Choose from a diverse range of restaurants befitting a town where half the population was born outside Canada. Add to that a fresh, hipster spin and – boom! – it's the West End. The top of the heap includes:

- Commoner (p123)
- Otto's Bierhalle (p122)
- Pizzeria Libretto (p123)

Union
FUSION $$

9 ✗ MAP P120, E5

This dandy little kitchen serves a delicious fusion of French- and Italian-inspired dishes that it touts as 'simple done right,' though you could argue that pickled swordfish with snow crab isn't simple. Fortunately, the food, decor and service are masterfully executed, using the freshest ingredients. Steak, chicken, ribs and fish are staples. There's a delightful patio out back. (☎416-850-0093; www.union72.ca; 72 Ossington Ave; mains $15-38; ⏰noon-3pm & 6-10pm Mon-Wed, to 11pm Thu & Fri, 11am-3pm & 6-11pm Sat, 6-10pm Sun; 🚋501)

Julie's Cuban
CUBAN $$

10 ✗ MAP P120, E5

Tucked on a residential block of the Little Portugal neighborhood, this joint serves Cuban tapas and traditional dishes such as *ropa vieja* (shredded beef in spicy tomato sauce with ripe plantains, white rice and black beans). The restaurant was once a mom-and-pop corner store, and every effort has been made to retain the vibe, with old photos, tchotchkes and twinkling lights. (☎416-532-7397; www.juliescuban.com; 202 Dovercourt Rd; tapas $4-15, mains $17-22; ⏰5:30-10pm Tue-Sun, closed Sun & Mon Nov-Apr; 🚋501)

Bang Bang Ice Cream
ICE CREAM $

11 ✗ MAP P120, F5

From burnt toffee to banana pudding, Bang Bang has more than two dozen house-made ice-cream flavours to try. Choose regular scoops, ice-cream sandwiches or bubble waffles with ice cream. Be prepared wait in a long line, especially in summer. (☎647-348-1900; http://bangbangicecream.ca; 93a Ossington Ave; scoops from $4.25; ⏰1-10pm Sun-Thu, to 10:30pm Fri & Sat; 👶; 🚋505)

Drinking

Bar Raval
BAR

12 🍺 MAP P120, H3

Standing in Bar Raval's magnificent, undulating mahogany interior, inspired by the works of Antoni Gaudí, feels like being surrounded by a set of petrified waves – it's otherworldly. The Basque-inspired *pinxtos* menu is the perfect complement to the surroundings: small sharing plates (squid in ink, smoked lamb belly, foie gras) go well with the list of layered cocktails and fine wines. (☎647-344-8001; www.thisisbarraval.com; 505 College St; ⏰11am-2am Mon-Fri, 10am-2am Sat & Sun; 🚋306, 506)

Bellwoods Brewery
BREWERY

13 🚋 MAP P120, E5

Fresh, urban-chic Bellwoods pours award-winning beers, from pale ales and double IPAs to stouts and wild ales. With candles lighting up the main room and gallery, the brewery itself is decidedly cool and buzzing with locals. An elevated menu of small plates – cheese boards, chicken-liver mousse, mussels – complements the beers. (www.bellwoodsbrewery.com; 124 Ossington Ave; ⊙2pm-midnight Mon-Wed, to 1am Thu & Fri, noon-1am Sat, to midnight Sun; 🚋505)

Gladstone Hotel
BAR

14 🚋 MAP P120, D5

This historic hotel revels in Toronto's avant-garde arts scene. The **Gladstone Ballroom** sustains offbeat DJs, poetry slams, jazz, book readings, alt-country and blues, and burlesque, while the **Melody Bar** hosts karaoke and other musical ventures. The cover varies, but is usually $10 or less. (📞416-531-4635; www.gladstonehotel.com; 1214 Queen St W; ⊙5pm-late Tue-Sat; 🚋501)

Drake Hotel
BAR

15 🚋 MAP P120, D6

The Drake is part boutique hotel, part pub, part live-music venue and part nightclub. There's a bunch of different areas to enjoy, including the chic **Sky Yard** rooftop bar and the hipster **Drake Underground** basement. Check the website for the lineup. (📞416-531-5042; www.thedrakehotel.ca; 1150 Queen St W; ⊙11am-2am Mon-Fri, 10am-am Sat-Sun; 🚋501)

Ossington
BAR

16 🚋 MAP P120, F5

With a moody candlelit front bar and a cavernous backroom hosting Friday and Saturday DJ nights, this local fave is a great mix of 20- to 30-somethings who still have a little life left in them and choose to stray from the mainstream mania. (📞416-850-0161; www.theossington.com; 61 Ossington Ave; cover $5; ⊙6pm-2am; 🚋501)

Local Experiences

Hanging out The 'it' street in the West End is Ossington Ave between Queen St W and Dundas St W – start your night at **Bellwoods Brewery** or the **Ossington**.

Community Packed on Tuesday nights, Choir! Choir! Choir! gets the whole bar at **Clinton's** (p127) singing rock songs, in harmony, by the end of the night. A fave.

Shopping Though there's great shopping on Queen St W, on summer weekends wander north toward Dundas for the terrific **yard sales** that pop up – there are many treasures to be found!

Henderson Brewing Company

BREWERY

17 MAP P120, B2

A laid-back warehouse brewery in the Junction Triangle neighborhood, Henderson has a tasting room with bar, picnic tables and huge fermentation tanks, offering views of staffers at work. Three beers (an amber, a lager and an IPA) are produced year-round; several others are created seasonally. Check the website for weekly events; there are pop-up eateries on weekends. (416-535-1212; https://hendersonbrewing.com; 128 Sterling Rd; 11am-10pm; 306, 506, S Lansdowne)

Après

WINE BAR

18 MAP P120, D6

Natural wine is what it's all about at minimalist Après. A small, ever-changing menu of shareable dishes pairs perfectly with the low-intervention and ethically farmed *vino* offered. (647-292-3317; www.apreswinebar.ca; 1166 Queen St W; 6pm-2am Tue-Thu, to 1am Fri & Sat, to midnight Sun; 501)

Snakes & Lattes

CAFE

19 MAP P120, H1

For a small cover fee, choose from over a thousand board games, along with local craft beers, milkshakes and shareable bites. Whether you're a Catan player or a Cards Against Humanity

SATE performs at the Dakota Tavern

fan, there's a game for everyone. Snakes & Lattes has a few storefronts across the city – this Bloor St location is especially popular with University of Toronto students. (☏647-342-9229; www.snakesandlattes.com; 600 Bloor St W; cover $8; ⏱11am-midnight Sun-Thu, to 2am Fri & Sat; 🛜 🚻; Ⓢ Bathurst)

Entertainment

Dakota Tavern — LIVE MUSIC

20 ⭐ MAP P120, F4

This basement tavern rocks, with wooden-barrel stools and a small stage where you can catch some twang. You'll hear mostly country and blues, plus a bit of rock. Sunday bluegrass brunches (adult/child $7/free; 10am to 2pm) are a *big* hit – they're tasty, filling and fun, but you'll have to queue to get in. (☏416-850-4579; www.facebook.com/TheDakotaTavern; 249 Ossington Ave; cover $10; ⏱8pm-2am Tue-Sun; 🚌63, 🚋501)

Theatre Centre — ARTS CENTER

21 ⭐ MAP P120, E6

Housed in a magnificent landmark building, the Theatre Centre produces and supports experimental works of performance and visual art. Come here to push your boundaries! (☏416-534-9261; http://theatrecentre.org; 1115 Queen St W; 🛜; 🚋501)

Open Roof Festival

An enthusiastic bunch of film- and music-lovers puts together a season of outdoor film screenings and bands for the **Open Roof Festival** (www.openrooffestival.com; $15; ⏱Jun-Aug; Ⓢ Dundas West) in an open lot in the up-and-coming Lower Junction neighborhood. Food trucks sell a variety of tasty treats.

Clinton's — LIVE PERFORMANCE

22 ⭐ MAP P120, G1

Weekly themed DJ nights, live music and comedy are all part of the lineup at iconic Clinton's, which attracts a fun, arty crowd. There's a pub at the front serving decent food and a wicked dance hall at the back. On Tuesday nights Choir! Choir! Choir! gets the entire audience singing well-known songs in three-part harmony. (☏416-535-9541; www.clintons.ca; 693 Bloor St; ⏱4pm-2am; Ⓢ Christie)

Mod Club — CONCERT VENUE

23 ⭐ MAP P120, F3

This excellent Little Italy venue showcases alt-rock acts like The Killers and Muse. If you want to flaunt your hip-hop rhymes, look out for 'trap karaoke.' On other nights, DJs play electronic, indie

West End Entertainment

West End Exploring

The West End is a highly walkable area, and the best way to experience it is to just wander and explore. Heading roughly east–west you'll pass from neighborhood to neighborhood, each with its own character and vibe. Lovely High Park marks the area's western edge. When you get tired of walking – it's a big part of town – there's plenty of public transit, especially along the main corridors, such as Queen and College Sts.

and Brit pop to a packed dance floor. Up-to-the-nanosecond lighting gives way to candlelit chill-out rooms. (416-588-4663; www.themodclub.com; 722 College St; 8pm-midnight Mon-Thu, 6pm-3am Fri & Sat; 506)

Shopping

House of Vintage
VINTAGE

24 MAP P120, C6

Fulfill your one-of-a-kind dreams at this perfectly curated vintage boutique in Parkdale. Known as one of Toronto's hottest spots for men's and women's unique and designer pieces, this place is bound to have something that fits the bill. (416-535-2142; http://houseofvintage-toronto.blogspot.com; 1239 Queen St W; noon-7pm Mon-Fri, 11am-7pm Sat, noon-6pm Sun; 501)

Craft Ontario Shop
ART

25 MAP P120, E6

Craft Ontario has been promoting the work of artisans in its gallery boutique for over 40 years. Ceramics, jewelry, glasswork, prints and carvings make up most of the displays, but you could also catch a special exhibition of Pangnirtung weaving or Cape Dorset graphics. Staff are knowledgeable about indigenous art. (416-921-1721; www.craftontario.com; 1106 Queen St W; 11am-6pm Mon, 10am-6pm Tue & Wed, to 7pm Thu-Sat, 11am-5pm Sun; 501)

Type Books
BOOKS

26 MAP P120, G6

A lovely independent bookstore with stenciled walls and chandeliers, Type has a little of everything for everyone. The laid-back vibe makes it easy to peruse the volumes (and even take a couple home!), and the colorful children's section is a gem. The whimsical knickknacks make good gifts, too. (416-366-8973; www.facebook.com/typebooks; 883 Queen St W; 10am-6pm Mon-Wed, to 7pm Thu-Sat, 11am-6pm Sun; 301, 501)

Public Butter Vintage
VINTAGE

27 MAP P120, C5

One of Toronto's most popular vintage stores, with everything from clothes to home decor. It's a little overwhelming when you walk in – so much stuff everywhere!

– but the odds are you'll find at least one item that you fancy. Plus, the prices are pretty darn good. (☏416-535-4343; http://publicbutter.com; 1290 Queen St W; ⊙11am-7pm Mon-Wed, to 8pm Thu & Fri, 10am-8pm Sat, 11am-6pm Sun; ◻501)

Châtelet HOMEWARES

28 🔒 MAP P120, H6

Meaning 'little castle' in French, Châtelet sells shabby-chic home goods with a country feel. You'll see everything from refurbished flea-market finds and vintage knickknacks to whitewashed furniture and whimsical tableware. It's a good place to pick up a decorative gift. (☏416-603-2278; 604 Queen St W; ⊙11am-6pm Mon, noon-6pm Tue-Sat, to 5pm Sun; ◻501)

Imperative CONCEPT STORE

29 🔒 MAP P120, C5

'All Vegan Everything' is the motto of this two-level boutique, selling clothes, shoes and accessories made sans animal products or exploitation. Many of the products are created by upscale Canadian brands, meaning you'll find high-quality items with flair. Decent prices, too. (☏416-551-7698; www.facebook.com/VeganImperative; 1332 Queen St W; ⊙noon-7pm Sun-Thu, 11am-7pm Fri & Sat; ◻501)

Imperative boutique

Toronto Designers Market DESIGN

30 🔒 MAP P120, A6

On the quiet westernmost end of Queen St, more than 30 small designers have set up mini studio-storefronts within a cavernous space. It's a mixed bag, but there are plenty of fresh ideas in the pop-ups, which sell jewelry, clothes, and gifts such as beard combs. (☏416-570-8773; www.torontodesignersmarket.com; 1605 Queen St W; ⊙11am-6pm Wed-Sun; ◻501)

West End Shopping

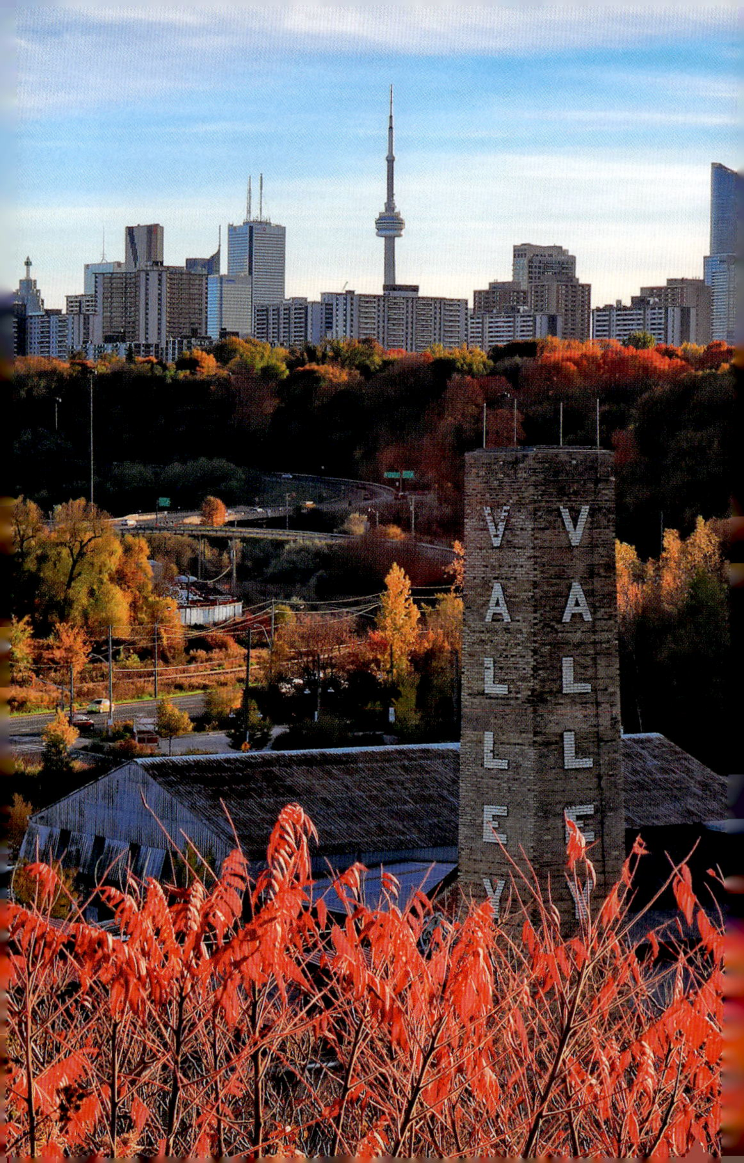
VALLEY
VALLEY

Explore
East Toronto & Rosedale

East Toronto is best known as a place to enjoy some greenery without leaving the city proper. It used to be a lush wilderness, fed by the Don River flowing through the glacier-carved Don Valley. Over time, the region became farmland, then a factory area and finally residential. Those previous identities – wild, agricultural, industrial – are evident in Evergreen Brick Works and Riverdale Farm. There's also a diverse cultural history in enclaves like Greektown and Little India, a tradition of arts and great food, and even a little hipster edge on Queen St E.

The Short List

- **Evergreen Brick Works (p132)** Exploring the verdant grounds and community spaces of this reclaimed brick quarry.

- **Rooftop (p140)** Sipping cocktails and soaking up the spectacular city views at this swanky hotel bar.

- **Riverdale Farm (p138)** Experiencing life – and chores – on a working farm that doubles as a family-friendly, hands-on museum.

- **Opera House (p141)** Rocking out to headliner concerts in a historic vaudeville performance space.

Getting There & Around

Streetcar 501, 502 and 503 connect downtown to Queen St E.

[S] The Green line runs along Danforth Ave, with several stops in East Toronto.

Neighborhood Map on p136

Evergreen Brick Works (p132) and a view of Toronto's skyline
CHARLINEXIA ONTARIO CANADA COLLECTION/ALAMY STOCK PHOTO ©

Top Sight
Evergreen Brick Works

An abandoned 1880s brick factory turned community gathering place, Evergreen Brick Works is an environmentally friendly complex that uses its various buildings and spaces to engage the city – there are art installations, live music, a farmers market, a kids' maker space, nature trails, event spaces and more. Come here to experience a slice of Toronto life.

◎ MAP P136, D1

www.evergreen.ca

550 Bayview Ave

free

⏲ 9am-5pm Mon-Fri, 8am-5pm Sat, 10am-5pm Sun

P 👥

🚌 28A, Ⓢ Broadview

Gathering Place

Among its many uses, Evergreen Brick Works is a gathering space. In summer there are guided nature walks and eco-focused workshops. Wednesday evenings bring food trucks, live music and art performances. In winter the ice rink opens, street curling is a must, and fire pits are lit for s'mores. On Saturdays a holiday market and cooking demonstrations keep things bustling.

Art Installations

Art is integrated into the public spaces here, most providing a commentary on Toronto's environment. Look for *Native Tenants*, giant native flowers 'growing' near the Children's Garden; *Deep Time,* in the Pavilions, depicting a glacial period 120,000 years ago; and, in Tiffany Commons, *Watershed Consciousness,* Toronto's largest living map, representing the city's ravine and river system.

Children's Garden

An inviting outdoor space, the Children's Garden draws kids in to explore and play. They'll find water features and sand, random loose parts, a garden and greenhouse, even a tipi and quiet zones. Each month there's a theme – waterways, gardening – though most play is self-directed. Staff members are also on hand to provide ideas and help.

Nature Trails

Don Valley Brick Works Park provides 16.5 hectares of outdoor space next to Evergreen Brick Works. Once a clay and shale quarry, it's now a forested park speckled with ponds and creeks, Carolinian trees and a wildflower meadow; trails and boardwalks run through it. For an uninterrupted skyline view of downtown Toronto, head to the top of the east slope.

★ Top Tips

○ The Children's Garden is only open to the public on weekends – plan accordingly!

○ Rent a bike on-site at Sweet Pete's Bike Shop.

○ Learn about the site's fascinating history through an archival photo wall tagged with historical graffiti.

○ Parking is in a self-pay lot – and yes, you'll get a ticket if you don't pay.

✕ Take a Break

Refuel at the **Sipping Container**, which serves craft beer and cider as well as organic coffee and fresh juices out of a repurposed – yup – shipping container.

If you want something more substantial, try **Café Belong**, an upscale lunch-and-dinner place featuring locally sourced ingredients.

Walking Tour

Cabbagetown & City Views

East Toronto used to be all forest and farmland, hugging the banks of the Don River. The area is fully urban today, yet with plenty of parks and green space. Our tour of the area ranges from Evergreen Brick Works, with its paths and eco-activities, to lovely Victorian-era homes and gourmet hors d'oeuvres at the swanky Rooftop bar.

Walk Facts

Start Allan Gardens Conservatory

End Rooster Coffee House

Length 2.8km; three hours

❶ Allan Gardens Conservatory

Begin at **Allan Gardens Conservatory** (p138), located in the oldest park in Toronto. Check out its domed glass ceiling, built in 1910, then continue into its 1500 sq meters of indoor botanical gardens of tropical flowers and rare plants (and warmth in winter).

❷ Cabbagetown

Continue east on **Carlton St**, admiring the change in architecture from modern apartment buildings to Victorian homes as you enter Cabbagetown, named for the cabbages Irish immigrants planted on their front lawns. At **Parliament St** take a left. Walk past little shops, markets and neighborhood restaurants in restored period buildings, and be sure to look up and around: murals are painted here and there on the redbrick walls. If you need a quick break, **Jet Fuel** (p141) is a good place for a coffee, **Salt & Tobacco** (p139) for a gourmet slice.

❸ Victorian Streetscapes

Take a right onto leafy **Winchester St**, admiring the well-preserved Victorian homes Cabbagetown is known for. This is said to be the largest continuous area of preserved Victorian housing in North America, and you'll see beautifully maintained homes in Gothic Revival, Bay & Gable, and Second Empire style sitting side by side, many with heritage plaques describing their histories. Explore **Metcalf St** and **Sackville St** for more Victorian streetscapes.

❹ Riverdale Farm

Meander back to Winchester, heading east until you hit **Riverdale Farm** (p138). A zoo for almost 100 years, it's now a working urban farm. Admission is free, so poke around the stables and fields, learn about pigs at a farmer demo, and maybe even help milk a goat!

❺ City Views

Head east on the farm, down to the foot bridge that crosses the Don River to verdant **Riverdale Park East**, with playing fields, benches and lots of open space. Climb to the top of the park – it's steep – to the charming **Rooster Coffee House** (p139). Turn around: you'll see one of the best skyline views in the city. Buy a brownie, take a load off, and enjoy the view.

East Toronto & Rosedale

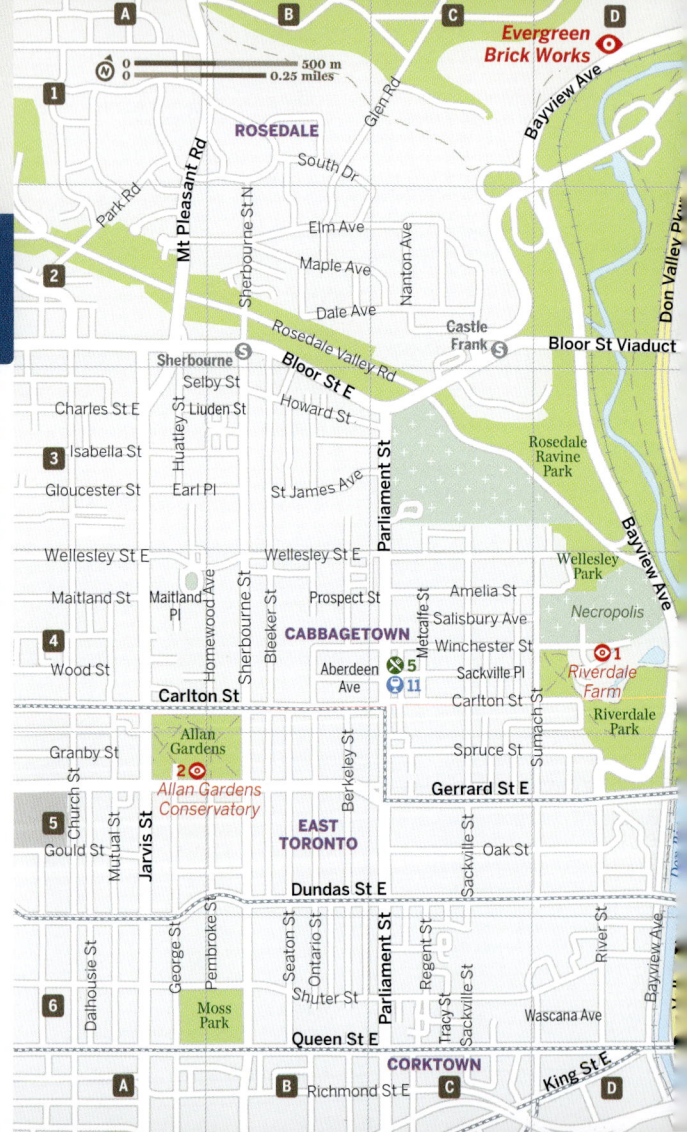

Map of East Toronto & Rosedale — page 136

Key locations:
- Evergreen Brick Works (D1)
- Allan Gardens Conservatory (A5)
- Riverdale Farm (D4)

Neighborhoods: Rosedale, Cabbagetown, East Toronto, Corktown

Notable streets and features:
- Mt Pleasant Rd, Park Rd, Glen Rd, Bayview Ave, Don Valley Pkwy
- South Dr, Elm Ave, Maple Ave, Dale Ave, Nanton Ave
- Rosedale Valley Rd, Bloor St E, Bloor St Viaduct
- Sherbourne (S), Castle Frank (S)
- Selby St, Linden St, Howard St, Charles St E, Isabella St, Gloucester St, St James Ave
- Wellesley St E, Maitland St, Maitland Pl, Prospect St, Amelia St, Salisbury Ave, Winchester St, Sackville Pl
- Wood St, Carlton St, Aberdeen Ave, Spruce St, Gerrard St E
- Granby St, Allan Gardens, Gould St, Dundas St E
- Oak St, Shuter St, Moss Park, Wascana Ave, Queen St E
- Richmond St E, King St E
- Rosedale Ravine Park, Wellesley Park, Necropolis, Riverdale Park

Streets (vertical): Church St, Jarvis St, Mutual St, Dalhousie St, George St, Pembroke St, Seaton St, Ontario St, Parliament St, Sherbourne St, Huntley St, Earl Pl, Homewood Ave, Bleeker St, Metcalfe St, Berkeley St, Sackville St, Regent St, Sumach St, Tracy St, River St

137

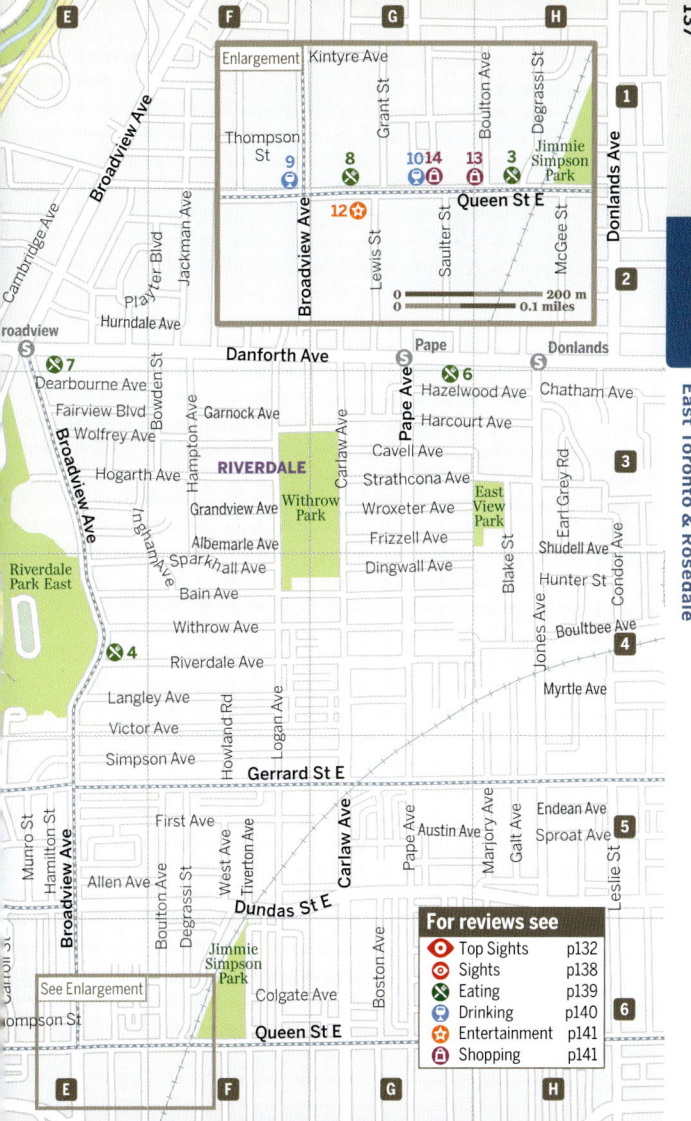

Enlargement

Kintyre Ave
Grant St
Boulton Ave
Degrassi St
Thompson St
9
8
10 14
13
3
Jimmie Simpson Park
Broadview Ave
Lewis St
Sauter St
McGee St
Queen St E
12

0 ——— 200 m
0 ——— 0.1 miles

Broadview Ave
Cambridge Ave
Playter Blvd
Jackman Ave
Hurndale Ave
Broadview
Danforth Ave
Pape
Donlands Ave

7
Dearbourne Ave
Hazelwood Ave
6
Chatham Ave
Fairview Blvd
Bowden St
Garnock Ave
Harcourt Ave
Wolfrey Ave
Hampton Ave
Cavell Ave
Hogarth Ave
Carlaw Ave
Strathcona Ave
East View Park
Earl Grey Rd
RIVERDALE
Grandview Ave
Withrow Park
Wroxeter Ave
Albemarle Ave
Frizzell Ave
Shudell Ave
Sparkhall Ave
Pape Ave
Blake St
Hunter St
Condor Ave
Ingham Ave
Bain Ave
Dingwall Ave
Riverdale Park East
Withrow Ave
Boultbee Ave
4
Riverdale Ave
Jones Ave
Langley Ave
Myrtle Ave
Victor Ave
Howland Rd
Logan Ave
Simpson Ave
Gerrard St E

First Ave
Austin Ave
Endean Ave
Hamilton St
Munro St
Allen Ave
West Ave
Tiverton Ave
Marjory Ave
Galt Ave
Sproat Ave
Boulton Ave
Degrassi Ave
Carlaw Ave
Pape Ave
Leslie St
Broadview Ave
Dundas St E

Jimmie Simpson Park
Boston Ave
Colgate Ave
See Enlargement
ompson St
Queen St E

For reviews see

🎯	Top Sights	p132
◎	Sights	p138
✖	Eating	p139
🍸	Drinking	p140
☆	Entertainment	p141
🔒	Shopping	p141

East Toronto & Rosedale

Sights

Riverdale Farm   MUSEUM

1 ⊙ MAP P136, D4

On the site of the Riverdale Zoo, where from 1888 to 1974 prairie wolves howled at night and spooked the Cabbagetown kids, Riverdale Farm is a downtown rural oasis. Now a working farm and museum, it has two barns, a summer wading pool, and pens of feathered and furry friends. Kids follow the farmers around as they do their daily chores, including milking goats and collecting eggs. Visitors can learn about a particular animal during the daily 'Farmer Demo' at 11:30am. From June to October there's also a Tuesday farmers market from 3pm to 7pm. (416-392-6794; http://riverdalefarm toronto.ca; 201 Winchester St; free; 9am-5pm; P; 506)

Allan Gardens Conservatory   GARDENS

2 ⊙ MAP P136, A5

Dating from 1858, Allan Gardens is one of Toronto's oldest parks. The highlight is its indoor botanical garden and conservatory, filled with plants from all around the world (and even some turtles in the orchid section). Housed in a stunning, historical cast-iron and glass building, it's a lovely little escape in the city, especially on a cold winter day. (416-392-7288; www.toronto.ca/explore-enjoy/parks-gardens-beaches/gardens-and-horticulture/conservatories/allan-gardens-conservatory; 160 Gerrard St E; free; 10am-4:45pm; 506)

Local Experiences

Happy hour

○ The **Rooftop** (p140) is *the* place to enjoy happy hour on the east side. Make reservations – yes, for a bar – or you'll have to wait till after dark.

Farmers market

○ Instead of heading to St Lawrence Market, east-siders shop for their fresh produce and artisanal cheeses at the **Evergreen Brick Works** (p132) farmers market.

Sledding

○ Riverdale Park East, in front of **Rooster Coffee House** (p139), is a popular spot to take a saucer or tube to shoot down its steep hills. Enjoy the view of downtown Toronto, if you can!

Eating

Bonjour Brioche FRENCH $

3 MAP P136, H1

The smell of freshly baked croissants will pull you into this little French bakery-cafe. Inside, a no-frills dining room bumps up against glass cases of picture-perfect, impossible-to-resist baked goods. Do yourself a solid: order a fresh salad, then dig into the chocolate brioche and croissants. Cash only. (416-406-1250; www.bonjourbrioche.com; 812 Queen St E; baked goods from $2.50, mains $8-12; 8am-4pm Mon-Sat; 501, 502, 503)

Rooster Coffee House CAFE $

4 MAP P136, E4

Set in a one-time general store, Rooster is a shabby-chic coffee shop known for its organic salads, sandwiches and great coffee. Street-side tables have the best city views around. No free seats? Take your treats and grab a bench in the park across the road. (416-995-1530; www.roostercoffeehouse.com; 479 Broadway Ave; snacks $3-11; 7am-8pm; 504, 505)

Salt & Tobacco PIZZA $

5 MAP P136, C4

A neighborhood pizzeria specializing in Roman-style pies, from the traditional (pepperoni and cheese) to the unusual (brussels sprouts and maple syrup). Gluten-free and vegan pizzas also on offer. Craft beers on tap and negronis just $5... what more is there to say? Diners eat at communal tables in the small, mid-century Modern space. (647-348-2993; www.saltandtobacco.com; 521 Parliament St; slices from $4, pizzas from $12; 11:30am-9pm Sun-Thu, to 9:30pm Fri & Sat;)

Athens GREEK $$

6 MAP P136, G3

As Greek as Greektown (aka the Danforth), modern and beachy Athens serves traditional dishes made with fresh, local ingredients: grilled calamari, lamb *kefte* (meatballs) and, of course, souvlaki. For a treat, try the moussaka and save room for walnut cake. Service is so friendly it feels like family...diners are even welcome in the kitchen to check out what's cooking! (416-465-4441; https://athensdanforth.ca; 707 Danforth Ave; dishes $8-33; 11am-midnight; S Donlands)

Summerlicious Toronto

Be sure to book your tables in advance for this **culinary extravaganza** (416-392-2489; www.toronto.ca/summerlicious; Jul), held at almost 200 restaurants, bars and cafes across the city. Great-value prix-fixe menus in three price categories mean there's something to suit most tastes and budgets.

Toronto Names Through Time

- Tkaronto
- Muddy York
- Toronto the Good
- Megacity
- The Centre of the Universe
- TO (pronounced 'Tee-Oh' or 'Tee-dot')
- The 416 (also 'the 6')

Allen's PUB FOOD $$
7 MAP P136, E2

Featuring one of the city's nicest patio dining areas (in warmer months), Allen's is more than just a pub, although it is a great place for lovers of Irish music and dance. The seasonal menu has hearty, sophisticated Irish fare: cuts of hormone- and additive-free beef, lamb, ale-battered halibut, and curries. (416-463-3086; www.allens.to; 143 Danforth Ave; mains $12-24; 11:30am-midnight Mon-Wed, to 1pm Thu & Fri, 10:30am-1am Sat, to midnight Sun; S Broadway, 504, 505)

Ruby Watchco CANADIAN $$$
8 MAP P136, G1

Creative farm-to-table comfort food is the game at this homey restaurant, run by two of Toronto's top chefs. (Chef Lynn even stars on the Food Network hit *Pitchin' In*.) A new menu is presented nightly, always four course, always prix fixe. Expect dishes like fried chicken with rosemary honey, and maple barbecue ribs; save room for the artisanal cheeses and decadent desserts. (416-465-0100; http://rubywatchco.ca; 730 Queen St E; prix fixe $58; 6-10pm Tue-Sat; 501, 502, 503)

Drinking

Rooftop ROOFTOP BAR
9 MAP P136, F1

This rooftop bar with floor-to-ceiling windows and a wraparound patio affords guests a 360-degree view of Toronto and a breathtaking outlook on the city skyline. Shareables and finger foods complement the cocktail and wine lists well. Sunsets are particularly busy. Reservations highly recommended. (416-362-8439; www.thebroadviewhotel.ca; Broadview Hotel, 106 Broadview Ave; 5pm-late Mon-Thu, 11:30am-late Fri-Sun; 501, 502, 503)

Comrade COCKTAIL BAR
10 MAP P136, G1

Reminiscent of a bygone era, the Comrade is a red-lit bar with a pressed-tin roof, mahogany accents and taxidermied animal heads hung high. The cocktail list is long and sophisticated, and the crowd mostly local. A good place to linger over a strong drink. (647-340-1738; www.thecomraderestaurant.com; 1124 Queen St E; 5:30pm-2am Mon-Thu, 5pm-2am Fri & Sat; 501, 502, 503)

Jet Fuel
COFFEE

11 MAP P136, C4

So arty and grungy, this hangout is for east-end gentrifiers, cyclists and literati who like to jeer at the beautiful people of Yorkville. The best coffee east of Yonge Street. (416-968-9982; www.jetfuelcoffee.com; 519 Parliament St; 6am-8pm; 506)

Entertainment

Opera House
CONCERT VENUE

12 MAP P136, G2

The old Opera House is an early-1900s vaudeville hall. Over the years, rockers like the Black Crowes, Rage Against the Machine, Eminem, Nirvana and Beck have all strutted out beneath the proscenium arch. Today, it's still considered one of the best small venues in town for concerts and DJ dance parties. (416-466-0313; www.theoperahousetoronto.com; 735 Queen St E; 501, 502, 503)

Shopping

Arts Market
ART

13 MAP P136, H1

A collective of local artists displays and sells work at this eclectic shop. High quality and unique, there's everything from handcrafted cards and jewelry to pottery and portraits. A few vintage finds, too. (416-778-9533; www.artsmarket.ca; 790 Queen St E;

Purchasing potatoes at Riverdale Farm (p138)

noon-5pm Mon-Thu, to 6pm Wed-Fri, 11am-6pm Sun; 501, 502, 503)

BRIKA
DESIGN

14 MAP P136, G1

A bright and airy boutique, BRIKA aims to inspire and create good mojo with its well-curated products, mostly home goods and beautiful accessories. What'll it be? A beautifully handcrafted messenger bag or a set of bath affirmations (test tubes filled with bath salts and daily mantras)? A perfect place to find a special gift or memento. (www.brika.com; 768 Queen St E; noon-5:30pm Mon-Wed, to 6pm Thu & Fri, 11am-6pm Sat & Sun; 501, 502, 503)

Worth a Trip 👓
Niagara Falls

An unstoppable flow of rushing water surges over the arcing fault in the riverbed with thunderous force. Great plumes of icy mist rise for hundreds of meters as the waters collide, like an ethereal veil concealing the vast rift behind the torrent. Thousands of onlookers delight in the spectacle every day, drawn by the force of the current and the hypnotic mist. This is Niagara Falls.

Table Rock Visitor Centre
📞 877-642-7275
www.niagaraparks.com
6650 Niagara Pkwy
🕘 9am-9pm, to 7pm Sep-May

Horseshoe Falls

The centerpiece of any visit here are the Horseshoe Falls (pictured). Named after their 670m curved shape, they have the highest flow rate of any waterfall in North America; at 65km/h, more than 2574 kiloliters of water per second crashes over the ridge into a roiling **Maid of the Mist Pool**. Powerful and playful, the turquoise waters mesmerize. The prime falls-watching spot is **Table Rock**, poised just meters from the drop – in the summer, arrive early to beat the crowds.

Bridal Veil & American Falls

Rushing waters between Luna and Goat islands create the Bridal Veil waterfall on the US side, just 17m wide. The falls form a perfect, full (and namesake) bridal-like veil that crashes onto mammoth rocks, 55m below. Next to it, the American Falls form an impressive 260m-wide curtain of rushing white water. During the day, rainbows often form in front of it.

The Skylon

The **Skylon Tower** (905-356-2651; www.skylon.com; 5200 Robinson St; adult/child $16.25/10.50; 9am-10pm Mon-Thu, to 11pm Fri-Sun; P) is a 158m concrete spire with yellow pill-shaped elevators crawling up and down the tower's neck to the top. The interior itself is dated, even a little sad, but the views! Eye-popping and simply picture perfect with the falls to the east and, on clear days, Toronto to the north. The two observation areas – a glass-enclosed indoor deck and a wire-fenced outdoor one – give you 360-degree views of the region. Plus, there's a revolving restaurant and a family-friendly buffet.

Hornblower Niagara Cruises

A classic Niagara Falls experience: **Hornblower boat tours** (www.niagaracruises.com; 5920 Niagara Pkwy; adult/child $26/16, fireworks cruise $40; 8:30am-8:30pm May-Sep, to 5:30pm Oct) come

★ Top Tips

○ The second floor of the Table Rock Visitor Centre is a little-known spot for great photos of Horseshoe Falls.

○ The **Niagara IMAX Theatre** offers excellent parking rates – around $10 per day – in front of the Skylon.

○ Niagara-on-the-Lake, one of the best-preserved 19th-century towns in North America, is just 25km from the falls.

✕ Take a Break

An iconic diner, **Flying Saucer** (Lundy's Lane; mains $7-27; 6am-1am Sun-Thu, to 2am Fri & Sat) offers classic eats in a saucer-shaped building.

A local favorite, **Koutouki** (http://koutoukiniagara.com; 5745 Ferry St; mains $22-42; 4-10pm Tue-Sun), serves classic Greek cuisine.

★ Getting There

Go Transit (p150) and VIA Rail (p150) offer return services to Niagara Falls from Toronto.

so close to the spectacular Bridal Veil Falls and Horseshoe Falls that you'll be drenched (despite the rain ponchos). Hornblower offers two tours on its 700-person catamarans: a 20-minute daytime 'Voyage to the Falls' and a 40-minute 'Fireworks Cruise' under the fireworks on summer nights with live music and cash bar. Avoid the massive ticket lines and buy a ticket online.

Summer Fireworks

A magnificent fireworks show takes place over the falls during the summer months: huge, sparkling lights and multicolored puffs light up the skies and the roaring falls below. The show starts at 10pm and is held nightly from June to August and on weekends in May, September and October. For a great view, stake out a spot near **Table Rock**, see it from the water on a Hornblower boat tour (p143), or head to the top of the Skylon (p143).

Botanical Gardens & Butterfly Conservatory

Forty hectares filled with thousands of perennials, sculpted shrubs and towering trees make the **Botanical Gardens** (905-356-8119; www.niagaraparks.com; 2565 Niagara Pkwy; butterfly conservatory adult/child $16/10.25, gardens free; 10am-4pm Mon-Fri, to 5pm Sat & Sun Sep-Jun, 10am-7pm Sun-Wed, to 8pm Thu-Sat Jul & Aug; P) a visually inspiring stop.

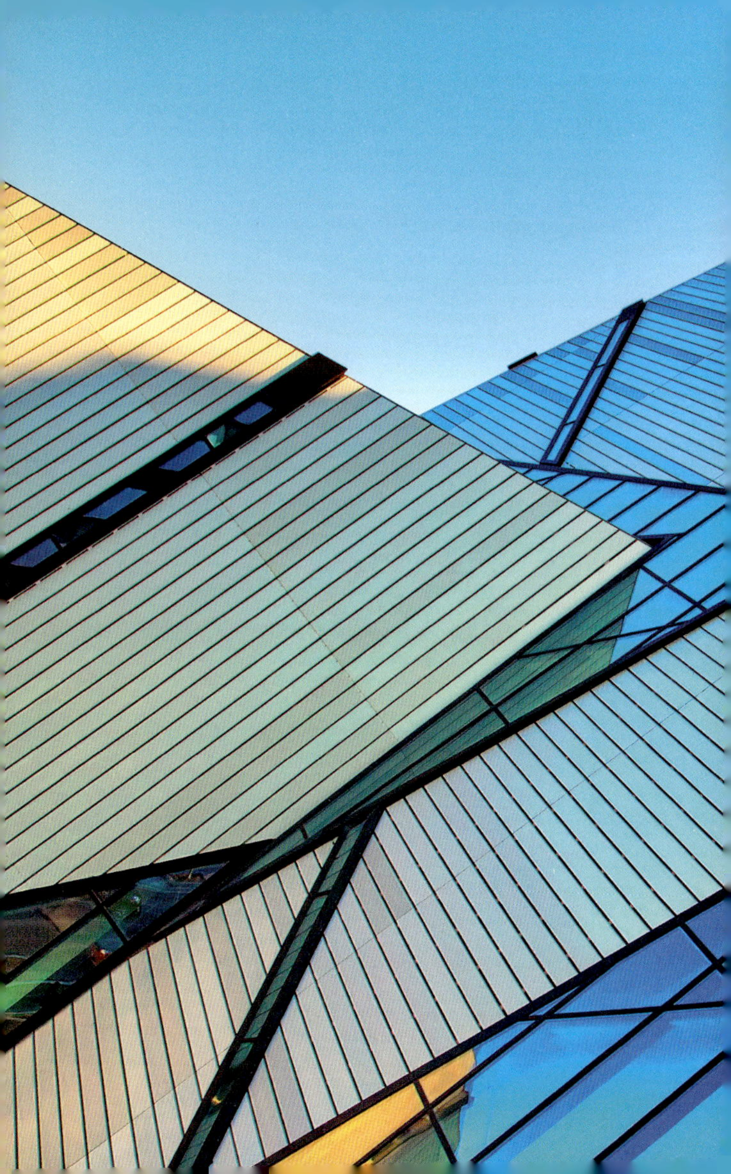

Niagara Falls and Hydroelectric Power

Though nowhere near the tallest waterfalls in the world (that honor goes to 979m Angel Falls in Venezuela), Niagara Falls is one of the world's most voluminous, with over 168,000 cubic meters of water going over its crest lines every minute. At least, that is, from 8am to 10pm during the peak tourist season of April to September.

In fact, the water making it over the falls – Horseshoe, American and Bridal Veil – only accounts for 25 to 50% of their capacity. The rest is diverted into hydroelectric plants on both sides of the border, depending on the time of day and year: Sir Andrew Beck Station Stations #1 and #2 in Ontario and Robert Moses Hydro Electric Plant in New York. Built across from each other, the hydroelectric plants divert water from the Niagara River using a system of gates 2.6km before the falls. The water is run through hydro tunnels on both sides of the border to turbines that generate electricity; the water is eventually returned to the Niagara River, just above Lake Ontario. The entire process is governed under the 1950 Niagara Treaty, an international agreement that assures water levels and a fair division of electricity (Ontario actually gets a little more). Power generated from the Niagara River accounts for 25% of all electricity used in Ontario and New York State – a remarkable figure, especially considering Toronto and New York City are included.

For visitors to Niagara Falls this means that, depending on the time of day and year, the falls may appear more or less voluminous. The highest volume any time of year is from April 1 to October 31, during daylight hours. The rest of the year, or at night, the falls look remarkably smaller but the street lights, somehow, seem to shine a little brighter.

Meander along the leafy paths, passing the parterre garden and the Victorian rose garden with more than 2400 roses. In the center, the domed **Butterfly Conservatory** houses a rainforest-like setting – plants, waterfalls, heat and more than 2,000 delicate butterflies flitting about, often landing on visitors.

Niagara Glen Nature Reserve

About 8km north of the falls is the exceptional **Niagara Glen Nature Reserve** (905-354-6678; www.niagaraparks.com; 3050 Niagara Pkwy; free; Reserve dawn-dusk, Nature Centre 10am-5pm Apr-Nov; P), where you can get a sense of what the area was like pre-Europeans. There are 4km of walking trails winding down into a gorge, past huge boulders, cold caves, wildflowers and woods. Park naturalists also offer daily one-hour guided nature walks (11am and 2pm; $7) during the summer season.

Survival Guide

Before You Go — 148
Book Your Stay — 148
When to Go — 148

Arriving in Toronto — 149

Getting Around — 150
Subway — 150
Streetcar — 150
Bus — 150
Boat — 150
Bike — 151
Taxi — 151
Car — 151

Essential Information — 152
Accessible Travel — 152
Business Hours — 152
Discount Cards — 152
Electricity — 153
Money — 153
Public Holidays — 153
Safe Travel — 154
Toilets — 154
Tourist Information — 154
Visas — 154

Exterior of the Royal Ontario Museum (p104)
ELIJAH LOVKOFF/ALAMY STOCK PHOTO ©; ARCHITECT: DANIEL LIBESKIND

Before You Go

Book Your Stay

- Toronto has a wide range of accommodations: high-rise hotels in the Financial and Entertainment Districts; boutique hotels in the West End; B&Bs in residential neighborhoods; and hostels that dot the city.
- Summer brings sold-out rooms at premium rates - book ahead!
- A 13% tax is added to room rates; occasionally an additional 3% destination tax is levied.

Useful Websites

Downtown Toronto Association of Bed and Breakfast Guest Houses (www.bnbinfo.com) Select listing of B&Bs.

Lonely Planet (lonelyplanet.com/canada/toronto/hotels) Recommendations and bookings.

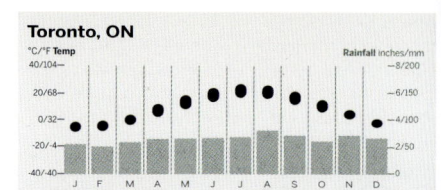

Toronto, ON

When to Go

- **Summer (Jun–Aug)** Enjoy gorgeous weather, patio dining and festival season in all its glory.
- **Autumn (Sep–Nov)** Visit for a cornucopia of fall colors and fewer crowds.
- **Winter (Dec–Feb)** Bundle up! Winter brings biting wind and snow but also hockey and outdoor ice skating.
- **Spring (Mar–May)** Celebrate the return of blue skies plus great deals on hotels.

Best Budget

Only Backpackers Inn (http://theonlyinn.com) Globetrotter fave with a relaxed vibe and loads of spaces for socializing.

Planet Travelers Hostel (www.theplanettraveler.com) Big, central hostel with a great rooftop lounge.

Hostelling International Toronto (www.hostellingtoronto.com) Youthful hostel with theme nights and a basement-level bar.

Two Peas Pod Hostel (www.twopeas.me) Rambling hostel with stacked 'pods' – wooden boxes with curtains and smart TVs – for bunks.

Clarence Park (www.theclarencepark.com) Modern hostel in a turn-of-the-century house overlooking a pleasant park.

Best Midrange

Anndore House (https://theanndorehouse.com) Stylish hotel with city views and a popular street-side patio.

Downtown Home Inn (www.downtownhomeinn.com) Pleasant row house repurposed into a cozy inn in Toronto's main LGBTIQ+ neighborhood.

Annex Hotel (https://theannex.com) Hipster hotel with feel-like-a-local features such as keyless entry and Netflix.

Cambridge Suites (www.cambridgesuitestoronto.com) All-suite hotel with kitchenettes and living rooms – perfect for longer stays.

Courtyard Toronto Downtown (www.marriott.com) Centrally located and comfortable chain hotel with frequent online deals.

Victoria's Mansion Inn & Guesthouse (www.victoriasmansion.com) All rooms have fridge, microwave and private bathroom, making the smaller singles decent downtown value.

Best Top End

Thompson Toronto (www.thompsonhotels.com/toronto) Chic, design-focused hotel with breathtaking skyline views.

Gladstone Hotel (www.gladstonehotel.com) Spectacular artist-designed rooms upstairs, and avant-garde arts and music scene downstairs.

Drake Hotel (www.thedrakehotel.ca) Artsy mid-century Modern hotel with popular rooftop and basement-level bars.

Four Seasons (www.fourseasons.com/toronto) Exquisite luxury hotel with stunning views and a relaxing vibe.

Hazelton (www.thehazeltonhotel.com) Sophisticated boutique hotel in one of Toronto's most exclusive neighborhoods.

Hotel X Toronto (http://hotelxtoronto.com) Stylish hotel with unbeatable waterfront and skyline views.

Arriving in Toronto

Toronto Pearson International Airport

Toronto International Airport (YYZ; http://torontopearson.com; 6301 Silver Dart Dr, Mississauga) Located 27km northwest of downtown. There are two terminals: 1 and 3. Check the website to confirm which one you'll be using to help with logistics. A free train connects the terminals as well as the Viscount Station, used by car-rental-agency shuttles.

Union Pearson Express (UP Express; www.upexpress.com; one way adult/child/family of 5 $12.35/free/25.70, one way on PRESTO card $9.25; ⌚ 5:30am-1am; 📶) Direct 25-minute rail to Union Station, stopping at Weston and Bloor stations. Traveling on a PRESTO card (p151) is highly recommended: the $6 rechargeable card pays for itself with a return trip to the airport and is useful for local transport.

Taxi Travel to downtown takes anywhere from 40 to 70 minutes, depending on traffic. Fares are $60 to downtown and $75 to destinations east of town.

Billy Bishop Toronto City Airport

Toronto Islands airport (YTZ; Map p34, A4; 📞 416-203-6942;

https://billybishopairport.com; 1 Island Airport, Centre Island; 🚋509) Home to smaller airlines, helicopter companies and private flyers. Convenient for regional travel.

Billy Bishop Airport Tunnel (Map p34, A3; www.billybishopairport.com; 🚋509) Looong moving walkways from Bathurst St to check-in counters take just six minutes.

Free ferry Shuttles passengers to the airport terminal in 90 seconds (5:30am to midnight).

Free shuttle bus Links Union Station to the ferry terminal and tunnel (5am to midnight Monday to Friday, 6:30am to 8:40pm Saturday, and 6:30am to midnight Sunday).

Union Station

Union Station (☎416-869-3000; https://torontounion.ca; 140 Bay St; Ⓢ Union, 🚋509, 510) Toronto's main transportation hub, home to:

VIA Rail (☎888-842-7245; www.viarail.ca) Plies the heavily trafficked Windsor–Montréal corridor and beyond.

Amtrak (www.amtrak.com) Provides long distance rail service including to Vancouver and New York City.

GO Transit (www.gotransit.com) Offers commuter rail and bus service to regional towns, including Niagara Falls.

Toronto Coach Terminal

Toronto Coach Terminal (Map p80, C6; ☎416-393-4636; 610 Bay St; Ⓢ Dundas) Toronto's long-distance bus terminal.

Greyhound Canada (https://greyhound.ca) Runs numerous domestic routes from here.

Megabus (https://ca.megabus.com) Has a smaller, and cheaper, selection of destinations.

Getting Around

Subway

- The fastest way to get across town, with two main lines: Green (Bloor–Danforth) and Yellow (Yonge–University–Spadina).
- One-way fare is $3.25/free per adult/child; two-hour transfers included.
- Service is from 6am (8am Sunday) until 1:30am daily.

Streetcar

- Extensive service throughout the city, though maddeningly slow during rush hour.
- Fare is $3.25/free per adult/child; two-hour transfers included.
- Runs 24 hours; service slows from 1:30am to 5am.

Bus

- Best for accessing areas outside Toronto's core.
- Fare is $3.25/free per adult/child; two-hour transfers included.
- Regular service is from 6am (8am Sunday) until 1am.
- Blue Night Network buses provide service on major bus routes from 1:30am to 5am daily (6am Saturday, 9am Sunday).

Boat

- From April to September **Toronto**

Public Transportation Tickets & Passes

o Tickets, tokens, day passes and PRESTO cards can all be used on the TTC ($3.25/free per adult/child); they include two-hour transfers.

o Tokens are discounted ($3) if you buy at least three.

o Day passes cost $13 and are good for unlimited travel until 5:30am the next day. On weekends, one day pass can be used by families or two adults. A great deal!

o A PRESTO card, a smart card storing credit, costs $6; convenient if you'll be using the TTC a lot, going to/from Toronto International Airport, or using GO Transit for day trips.

o Check the TTC website (www.ttc.ca) for maps and timetables.

Islands Ferries (Map p34, E3; ☎416-392-8193; www.toronto.ca; 9 Queens Quay W; adult/child return $8.19/3.95; **S** Union) run to Centre Island (8am to 11:15pm), Hanlan's Point (6:30am to 10pm Monday to Friday, 8am to 10:45pm Saturday and Sunday) and Ward's Island (6:35am to 11:15pm).

o From October to March, ferries only run to Ward's Island and Hanlan's Point.

o Return fare is $8.19/3.95 per adult/child.

o Book online (www.toronto.ca) to skip the purchase queue.

o **Tiki Taxi** (☎647-347-8454; www.tikitaxi.ca; 441 Queens Quay W; adult/child $10/5; ⊙9am-9pm Mon-Fri, 8am-9pm Sat & Sun; ☐310, 509, 510) provides water-taxi service to the Islands. One-way fare is $10 per person. It departs when full.

Bike

o **Bike Share Toronto** (☎855-898-2378; www.bikeshareto ronto.com) A city-wide bike-share program that rents bikes in 30-minute increments, either for a single use ($3.25) or for unlimited periods using one- and three-day passes ($7/15). Prepare to pay a premium if you fail to dock your bike every 30 minutes!

o Rentals are around $15/35 per hour/day; bike shops are along the waterfront.

o City buses have easily loadable bike racks; first come, first served.

o Bikes are permitted on streetcars and subway trains during off-peak hours only (before 6:30am, between 10am and 3:30pm, and after 7pm weekdays, and all weekend).

Taxi

o Easily hailed downtown; also line up outside big hotels.

o Metered fares start at $4.25, plus $1.75 per kilometer, depending on traffic.

o A tip of 15% to 20% is customary.

Car

o Driving downtown is not recommended due to relentless traffic and construction.

o Parking is usually $3 to $4 per half-hour in a private lot; reduced-rate parking is often offered before 7am and after 6pm.

- Public lots and street parking are $1.50 to $4 per hour, depending on the neighborhood.

Essential Information

Accessible Travel

Download Lonely Planet's free Accessible Travel guides from http://lptravel.to/AccessibleTravel.

TTC buses are all low-floor accessible, and have tools for the vision and hearing impaired. Few streetcars are accessible to the mobility impaired: the 509 and 510 lines are the only routes that accommodate everyone. And only half of the subway stations have elevators.

Lodging is a similarly mixed bag: Modern hotels tend to have elevators, and wider doors and bathrooms, while smaller hotels and B&Bs, many in refurbished Victorians, often do not.

Wheelchair Accessible Taxi Service (https://wheelchairtaxi.online) Provides door-to-door service to the mobility impaired in the Greater Toronto Area.

Access to Travel (www.accesstotravel.gc.ca) Proves information on accessible transportation and travel across Canada.

Society for Accessible Travel & Hospitality (www.sath.org) Tips and blogs for travelers with disabilities.

Business Hours

Opening hours are generally shorter in the shoulder and low seasons.

Banks 8am to 5pm Monday to Friday; some open 9am to noon Saturday

Restaurants breakfast 7am to 11am, lunch 11am to 3pm, dinner 5pm to 10pm; some open for brunch 8am–1pm Saturday and Sunday

Bars noon to midnight Sunday to Wednesday, to 2am Thursday to Saturday

Clubs 9pm to 3am Thursday to Saturday

Shops 10am to 7pm Monday to Thursday, to 9pm Friday to Saturday, noon to 5pm Sunday

Supermarkets 7am to 10pm; some open 24 hours

Discount Cards

Toronto CityPASS (www.citypass.com/toronto; adult/child

Dos & Don'ts

Torontonians are a fairly laid-back, friendly crowd and aren't easily offended; however, some rules of etiquette do apply:

Courtesy Please, thank you, and sorry are highly valued words. Use them. Please.

Patriotism Canadians are very proud of their nationality – avoid commenting that they are pretty much just Americans.

Queues While Torontonians usually tut when dismayed, cutting a line can prompt full-on shouts.

Shoes Remove your footwear and place it in the area provided in B&Bs and homes.

$73/50) One price for five attractions: the CN Tower, Ripley's Aquarium of Canada, the Royal Ontario Museum, Casa Loma and your choice of the Ontario Science Centre or Toronto Zoo. A good deal if you go to at least three.

International Student Identity Card (www.isic.org) Provides students with discounts on travel insurance and admission to museums and other sights. Cards also available for those under 26 but not students, and for full-time teachers.

Electricity

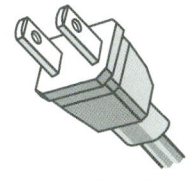

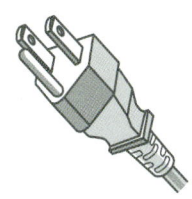

Type A
120V/60Hz

Type B
120V/60Hz

Money

The Canadian dollar ($) is the local currency.

ATMs

ATMs are widely available in Toronto. Look for international networks like Cirrus, Plus, Star and Maestro to ensure that your ATM, credit or debit cards will work.

Scotiabank (www.scotiabank.com) provides no-fee ATM withdrawals for members of the Global ATM Alliance. Your own bank, however, might still charge you a fee.

Many convenience-store ATMs charge an additional machine fee, typically $2 to $5.

Credit Cards

Major credit cards such as MasterCard, Visa and American Express are accepted just about everywhere. The exceptions are mom-and-pop shops and small markets, mostly in Kensington Market and Chinatown, which are cash only.

Changing Money

To exchange cash, tackle the banks or try **Money Mart** (www.moneymart.ca; 617 Yonge St; 24hr; [S] Wellesley).

Public Holidays

Several public holidays shut down banks, schools, government offices and often many private businesses:

New Year's Day January 1

Family Day Third Monday in February

Good Friday March or April

Money-saving Tips

- Many festivals are free or pay-what-you-can. Exceptions include film and food festivals.
- Most museums offer free days every month and discounted admission for kids every day.
- Reduced price tickets to the symphony, ballet and opera are often available for anyone under 30.
- Rush tickets to big ticket shows are sold same day and go fast – plan accordingly!

Easter Monday March or April

Victoria Day Third Monday in May

Canada Day July 1

Civic Day First Monday in August

Labour Day First Monday in September

Thanksgiving Second Monday in October

Remembrance Day November 11

Christmas Day December 25

Boxing Day December 26

Safe Travel

By North American standards, Toronto is a safe city to live in and to visit, but be aware of the following:

- Yonge St can be sketchy, especially heading north toward Bloor as the strip clubs, sex shops and bars increase in density. Be aware of your surroundings and avoid walking alone at night. Alternatively, walk on University Ave, just west of Yonge.
- At night, Cabbagetown South – particularly around Allan Gardens and George St – is iffy. Best take a cab or ride share.

Toilets

- Private businesses usually only allow customers to use washrooms and often have a key to enforce this.
- Shopping malls such as the Eaton Centre, and tourist complexes like the Harbourfront Centre, Distillery District and St Lawrence Market, have free public washrooms.

Tourist Information

Ontario Travel Information Centre (Map p48, G4; 416-314-5899; www.ontariotravel.net; Union Station, 65 Front St W; 9am-6pm Mon-Sat, 10am-6pm Sun; S Union) Knowledgeable multilingual staff and overflowing racks of brochures that cover every nook and cranny of Toronto and beyond.

Visas

Visitors to Canada must hold a valid passport with at least six months remaining before its expiration. Visitors from visa-exempt countries (with the exception of the USA) are required to purchase an Electronic Travel Authorization (eTA; $7), before departing their home country. Visitors from non-visa-waiver countries must apply for the appropriate visa prior to arriving in Canada. For more info, check the website of **Citizenship & Immigration Canada** (www.cic.gc.ca).

Behind the Scenes

Send Us Your Feedback

We love to hear from travelers – your comments help make our books better. We read every word, and we guarantee that your feedback goes straight to the authors. Visit **lonelyplanet.com/contact** to submit your updates and suggestions.

Note: We may edit, reproduce and incorporate your comments in Lonely Planet products such as guidebooks, websites and digital products, so let us know if you don't want your comments reproduced or your name acknowledged. For a copy of our privacy policy visit lonelyplanet.com/privacy.

Liza's Thanks

A shout out to the extraordinary LP team: Ben Buckner, the production crew, my co-authors – I'm so proud to be able to work with you. *Mil gracias* to Mom and Dad for your boundless support, love, and curiosity about places so close to home. Big thanks to Eva and Leo for waiting so patiently for 'Fun… With Mom.' And Gary, my love, there is absolutely no way I could do my job without you. Your support, your understanding, your cheerleading. Thank you, always.

Acknowledgements

Cover photograph: View of Toronto's skyline from the Harbourfront, Javen/Shutterstock ©

This Book

This 1st edition of Lonely Planet's *Pocket Toronto* guidebook was curated, researched and written by Liza Prado. This guidebook was produced by the following:

Destination Editor
Ben Buckner

Senior Product Editors
Martine Power, Saralinda Turner

Regional Senior Cartographer
Corey Hutchison

Product Editor
Jenna Myers

Book Designer
Meri Blazevski

Assisting Editors Joel Cotterell, Peter Cruttenden, Sarah Bailey, Vicky Smith, Gabrielle Stefanos

Cover Researcher
Naomi Parker

Thanks to Alison Ridgway, Angela Tinson

Index

See also separate subindexes for:
- Eating p158
- Drinking p159
- Entertainment p159
- Shopping p159

401 Richmond 50

A

accessible travel 152
accommodations 148-9
air travel 149-50
Allan Gardens Conservatory 138
American Falls 143
Annex, the 103-15, **106-7**
 drinking 112-13
 entertainment 113, 115
 food 110-12
 local life 113
 shopping 115
 sights 108-9
 transportation 103
architecture 46-7, 93
 Victorian 135
Art Gallery of Ontario 92-3
arts 93, 105, 133
ATMs 153

B

Bata Shoe Museum 108
bathrooms 154

Sights 000
Map Pages **000**

bicycle travel 151
boat tours 33, 143-4
boat travel 150-1
Botanical Gardens 144-5
breweries 14
Bridal Veil Falls 143
bus travel 150
business hours 152
Butterfly Conservatory 145

C

Cabbagetown 134-5, **134**
Canadian National Exhibition 39
car travel 151-2
Casa Loma 108
cell phones 22
changing money 153
children, travel with 18
Children's Garden 133
Chinatown 91-101, **94-5**
 drinking 98-9
 entertainment 99-100
 food 96-8
 local life 98
 shopping 100-1
 sights 92-3
 transportation 91

Christmas Market 70
Church of the Holy Trinity 82
cinemas 13
City Hall 82
climate 148
CN Tower 44-5, 47
Corktown 59-71, **64**
 drinking 68-9
 entertainment 69-70
 food 66-8
 itineraries 62-3, **62**
 local life 68
 shopping 70-1
 sights 65-6
 transportation 59
 walks 62-3, **62**
costs 22, 57, 154
credit cards 153
currency 22
cycling 151

D

dangers, see safety
David Pecault Square 47
Design Exchange 47, 51
disabilities, travelers with 152
discount cards 17, 152-3

Discovery Gallery 105
Distillery District 59-71, **64**
 drinking 68
 entertainment 69-70
 itineraries 62-3, **62**
 local life 68
 shopping 70-1
 sights 65
 transportation 59
 walks 62-3, **62**
Don Valley Brick Works Park 133
Doors Open Toronto 84
Downtown Yonge 75-89, **80-1**
 drinking 86-8
 entertainment 88
 food 82-5
 local life 83
 shopping 88-9
 sights 76-9, 82
 transportation 75
drinking 14, see also individual neighborhoods, Drinking subindex

E

East Toronto 131-41, **136-7**
 drinking 140-1
 food 139-40

itineraries 134-5, **134**
local life 138
sights 132-3, 138
transportation 131
walks 134-5, **134**
EdgeWalk 45
electricity 153
Elgin Theatre 76-9
entertainment 12-13, *see also individual neighborhoods*, Entertainment subindex
Entertainment District 43-57, **48-9**
drinking 54-5
entertainment 55-7
food 51-4
itineraries 46-7, **46**
local life 54
shopping 57
sights 44-5, 50-1
transportation 43
walks 46-7, **46**
etiquette 152
events 31, *see also festivals*
Evergreen Brick Works 132-3
Exhibition Place 39

F

Family Gallery of Hands-on Biodiversity 105
festivals 15, 31, 53, 70, 87, 100, 127, 139
film industry 114
Financial District 43-57, **48-9**
drinking 54-5
entertainment 55-7
food 51-4
itineraries 46-7, **46**

local life 54
shopping 57
sights 44-5, 50-1
transportation 43
walks 46-7, **46**
First Nations 86
art 93
Flatiron Building 63, 65-6
food 10-11, 66, *see also individual neighborhoods*, Eating subindex
festivals 15, 53, 139
tours 11
Fort York National Historic Site 33, 36
free attractions 17

G

Galleria Italia 93
Gardiner Museum 108
gay travelers 19, 87
Grafitti Alley 50

H

Hanlan's Point Beach 41
Harbourfront Canoe & Kayak Centre 37
Harbourfront Centre 30-1, 33
Henry Moore Sculpture Centre 93
Heritage Toronto 110
High Park 118-19
highlights 6-9
history 140
artifacts 108
First Nations 86
Hockey Hall of Fame 47, 50

holidays 153-4
Horseshoe Falls 143
Hot Docs 114
HTO Waterfront Parks 33
hydroelectric power 145

I

Inside Out 114
internet resources 13, 148
itineraries 20-1, *see also individual neighborhoods*

K

Kensington Market 91-101, **94-5**
drinking 98-9
entertainment 99-100
food 96-8
local life 98
shopping 100-1
transportation 91

L

languages 22
LGBTIQ+ travelers 19, 87
live music 12

M

Market Gallery 61
Market Kitchen 61
markets 16
Martin Goodman Trail 33, 37
mobile phones 22
money 22, 154
murals 63, 77
Museum of Contemporary Art Toronto 122

N

Native Canadian Centre of Toronto 109
Natrel Rink 36-7
Nature Centre 119
nature trails 73, 133
Niagara Falls 142-5, 144
Niagara Glen Nature Reserve 145
nightlife 14, *see also individual neighborhoods*, Drinking subindex

O

Old Town 59-71, **64**
drinking 68-9
entertainment 69-70
food 66-8
itineraries 62-3, **62**
local life 68
shopping 70-1
sights 60-1, 65-6
transportation 59
walks 62-3, **62**
Olympic Island 41
opening hours 152

P

planning 22
Power Plant Contemporary Art Gallery 31, 35
PRESTO card 151
Pride Toronto 87
public holidays 153-4
public transportation tickets & passes 151

Q

Queen's Quay Terminal 33

R

Ripley's Aquarium of Canada 47, 50
Riverdale Farm 135, 138
Riverdale Park East 135
Rogers Centre 47, 51
ROMBus 109
Rosedale 131-41, **136-7**
 drinking 140-1
 food 139-40
 itineraries 134-5, **134**
 local life 138
 sights 138
 transportation 131
 walks 134-5, **134**
Roy Thomson Hall 47
Royal Ontario Museum 104-5

S

safety 154
Saturday Farmers Market 61, 63
Shakespeare in High Park 119
shopping 16, see also individual neighborhoods, Shopping subindex
Simcoe Park 47
Skylon Tower 143
Spadina Museum 109
Spadina Quay Wetlands 36
St Lawrence Hall 63

St Lawrence Market Complex 60-1
St Lawrence Market South 63
stand-up paddleboarding 41
street art 99
streetcars 150
subway travel 150
Sugar Beach Park 36
Sunday Antique Market 61, 63

T

Tall Ship Kajama 38
taxis 151
Textile Museum of Canada 82
theater 12
time 22
tipping 22
toilets 154
Tommy Thompson Park 72-3
top sights 6-9
Toronto International Film Festival 114
Toronto Island SUP 41
Toronto Islands 40-1
Toronto Light Festival 70
Toronto Music Garden 33, 35
Toronto's First Post Office 66
tourist information 154
tours
 boat 33, 143-4
 food 11
 free 17
 walking 110
train travel 150
transportation 23, 149-52
TTC 151

U

Union Station 47, 150
Union Summer 53

V

viewpoints 73, 135
visas 154

W

walks 73, 110, 119, 128, 133, see also individual neighborhoods
Ward's Island Beach 41
Waterfront 29-39, **34**
 drinking 39
 food 38-9
 itineraries 32-3, **32**
 local life 36
 sights 30-1, 35-9
 transportation 29
 walks 32-3, **32**
weather 148
websites 13, 148
West End 117-29, **120-1**
 drinking 124-7
 entertainment 127-8
 food 122-4
 local life 125
 shopping 125, 128-9
 sights 118-19, 122
 transportation 117
Wheel Excitement 38
wildlife 119
Winter Garden Theatre 76-9

Y

Yorkville 103-15, **106-7**
 drinking 112-13
 entertainment 113, 115

 food 110-12
 local life 113
 shopping 115
 sights 104-5, 108-9
 transportation 103
Young Centre for the Performing Arts 63

✖ Eating

AGO Bistro 93
Allen's 140
Annex Food Hall 110
Assembly Chef's Hall 52
Athens 139
Aunties & Uncles 110
Bang Bang Ice Cream 124
Bonjour Brioche 139
Boxcar Social 38-9
Buca 53
Café Belong 133
Café Cancan 112
Chef's House 67
Commoner 123
DaiLo 123
Dipped Donuts 98
Druxy's ROM Café 105
FIKA Cafe 97-8
Forno Cultura 54
Fuwa Fuwa 110-11
Gale's Snack Bar 73
Grand Electric Parkdale 122
Grenadier Café 119
Hair of the Dog 85
Harbord Bakery 110
Harbour 60 39
House of Gourmet 96
Julie's Cuban 124
Kekou 98
Lee 53
Loblaw's 83

Los Guaca-Moles 122
Mother's Dumplings 97
Mr Tonkatsu 111
Nami 68
Nguyen Huong 97
NishDish 122-3
Okonomi House 83
Otto's Bierhalle 122
Outdoor Eateries 82-3
Pai 52
Parka Food Co. 96
Patrician Grill 66
Patties Express 83
Pearl Diver 67-8
Piano Piano 112
Pizzeria Libretto 123
Pow Wow Café 97
Queen's Quay Terminal 39
Ravi Soups 51-2
Richmond Station 53
Riviera 41
Rooster Coffee House 139
Ruby Watchco 140
Salad King 84
Salt & Tobacco 139
Sassafraz 112
Schnitzel Queen 66
Senator Restaurant 84-5
Seven Lives 97
Smith 84
Sushi on Bloor 111
Swatow 97
Trattoria Nervosa 112
Union 124
Urban Eatery 84
VUE Bistros 45
Wilbur Mexicana 52
Wish Restaurant 85

WORKS Gourmet Burger Bistro 67

🍷 Drinking

Against the Grain Urban Tavern 39
Après 126
Bar Raval 124
BarChef 98-9
Bellwoods Brewery 125
Black Eagle 87
C'est What 68
Comrade 140
Crews & Tangos 87
Drake Hotel 125
Espresso Bar 93
Fifth Social Club 55
Gladstone Hotel 125
Handlebar 99
Henderson Brewing Company 126
Jet Fuel 141
Jimmy's 54
Madison Avenue Pub 113
Mill Street Brewery 68
Moonbean Coffee Company 99
O'Grady's 86
One Eighty 87
Ossington 125
Oxley 112-13
Petty Cash 55
Rooftop 140
Rorschach Brewing Co 73
Sipping Container 133
Slanted Door 113
Snakes & Lattes 126-7
Storm Crow Manor 87

Thompson Toronto 54
Triple A Bar 69
Underground Garage 55
Velvet Underground 99
Woody's/Sailor 88

🎭 Entertainment

Adelaide Hall 56
Buddies in Bad Times Theatre 88
Cameron House 100
Canadian Opera Company 56
CanStage 70
Clinton's 127
Dakota Tavern 127
Ed Mirvish Theatre 88
Factory Theatre 56
Horseshoe Tavern 99
Hot Docs Ted Rogers Cinema 113-15
Lee's Palace 115
Massey Hall 88
Mod Club 127-8
Opera House 141
Reservoir Lounge 69
Rex 100
Royal Alexandra Theatre 56
Scotiabank Arena 57
Second City Toronto 55
Soulpepper 69-70
Theatre Centre 127
Theatre Passe Muraille 100
TIFF Bell Lightbox 55
Toronto Symphony Orchestra 56
Young People's Theatre 70

🛍 Shopping

Arts Market 141
Bay of Spirits Gallery 101
Ben McNally 57
BMV 115
BRIKA 141
Bungalow 101
Châtelet 129
Corktown Designs 71
Courage My Love 100
Craft Ontario Shop 128
Dead Dog Records 89
Eaton Centre 89
Freshly Baked Tees 57
Gallery Indigena 71
Glad Day 88
Harbourfront Centre Shop 31
Hoi Bo 70-1
House of Vintage 128
Imperative 129
MEC 101
Mink Mile 115
Out on the Street 89
Outer Layer 57
Page & Panel: The TCAF Shop 115
Pink Tartan 115
Public Butter Vintage 128-9
Sonic Boom 100-1
Spacing Store 57
Toronto Designers Market 129
Type Books 128

Our Writer

Liza Prado

Liza Prado has been a travel writer since 2003, when she made a move from corporate lawyering to travel writing (and never looked back). She's written dozens of guidebooks and articles, as well as apps and blogs to destinations throughout the Americas. She takes decent photos, too. Liza is a graduate of Brown University and Stanford Law School. She lives very happily in Denver, Colorado, with her husband and fellow Lonely Planet writer, Gary Chandler, and their two kids.

Published by Lonely Planet Global Limited
CRN 554153
1st edition – Feb 2020
ISBN 978 1 78868 338 8
© Lonely Planet 2020   Photographs © as indicated 2020
10 9 8 7 6 5 4 3 2 1
Printed in Singapore

Although the authors and Lonely Planet have taken all reasonable care in preparing this book, we make no warranty about the accuracy or completeness of its content and, to the maximum extent permitted, disclaim all liability arising from its use.

All rights reserved. No part of this publication may be copied, stored in a retrieval system, or transmitted in any form by any means, electronic, mechanical, recording or otherwise, except brief extracts for the purpose of review, and no part of this publication may be sold or hired, without the written permission of the publisher. Lonely Planet and the Lonely Planet logo are trademarks of Lonely Planet and are registered in the US Patent and Trademark Office and in other countries. Lonely Planet does not allow its name or logo to be appropriated by commercial establishments, such as retailers, restaurants or hotels. Please let us know of any misuses: lonelyplanet.com/ip.